OVER IT

A TEEN'S GUIDE TO GETTING BEYOND OBSESSIONS WITH FOOD AND WEIGHT

CAROL EMERY NORMANDI & LAURELEE ROARK

NEW WORLD LIBRARY
NOVATO, CALIFORNIA

New World Library
14 Pamaron Way
Novato, California 94949

The material in this book is intended for education. It is not meant to take the place of diagnosis and treatment by a qualified medical practitioner or therapist. No expressed or implied guarantee as to the effects of the use of the recommendations can be given nor liability taken.

Some of the personal stories in this book have been changed to protect the confidentiality of the individuals.

Grateful acknowledgment is made to the following for permission to use the following material: The exercise appearing on page 94 reprinted from Carol Emery Normandi and Laurelee Roark, *It's Not About Food* (New York: Perigee Books, 1998). Used by permission of Penguin Putnam, Inc. Excerpt from "Saint Francis and the Sow" from THREE BOOKS by Galway Kinnell. Previously published in *Mortal Acts, Mortal Words* (1980). Reprinted by permission of Houghton Mifflin. All Rights Reserved.

Library of Congress Cataloging-in-Publication Data

Normandi, Carol Emery.
Over it : a teen's guide to getting beyond obsessions with food and weight / by Carol Emery Normandi & Laurelee Roark.
    p.   cm.
Includes bibliographical references and index.
ISBN 1-57731-148-5
1. Eating disorders in adolescence—Juvenile literature. 2. Eating disorders—Patients—Juvenile literature. 3. Teenagers—Mental health—Juvenile literature. I. Roark, Laurelee. II. Title.

RJ506.E18 N67 2001
616.85'26'00835—dc21   00-011139

First Printing, March 2001
ISBN 1-57731-148-5
Printed in Canada on acid-free paper
Distributed to the trade by Publishers Group West
10 9 8 7 6 5 4 3 2 1

To fat girls, thin girls, tall girls, short girls, large girls, small girls, round girls, and straight girls everywhere — may you rejoice in your uniqueness and stop the cycle of body hatred for generations to come.

Contents

by Kate Dillon

I'm not sure how many things I believe I truly know. I mean really know. But I know I'm right about this one thing. I first knew it when I was twenty-one years old, and by the time I was twenty- two, my knowledge was like an army of revolutionaries ready to die for their truth! My truth is that I am free. I am free from cultural ideals, and anyone or anything trying to inflict these ideals upon me. I am free to be whomever I want or need to be at any given moment — beautiful, ugly, fat, thin, smart, goofy, cool, or really uncool. I am free to make mistakes, to say the wrong things, to do everything, or to do nothing at all. I know I'm free now because for seven years I wasn't free at all. I lived in a remote and lonely place, confined by anorexia, sentenced by myself.

I made a conscious decision to become anorexic when I was twelve years old. I'd just started junior high, and subsequently learned that I was "fat and ugly." My peers christened me "Overweight Kate," and they'd chant it on the school bus or just say it straight to my face. Ironically, I learned about anorexia from a made-for-TV movie attempting to inform its viewers of the horrors of eating disorders. The fact that the anorexic girl died in the movie made less of an impression on me than the fact that I now had a solution to the problem I was having at school. I figured if I were skinny they wouldn't be able to tease me anymore.

Unfortunately, my "solution" worked quite well, and when I was sixteen I signed with Elite Model Management, beginning a lucrative and glamorous career in fashion. After graduating from high school, I moved to New York City and then Paris to work full time. Some of it was as idyllic as one would imagine. I worked for the best magazines with the best photographers and traveled all over the world. I had an apartment in Paris and an apartment in New York. The celebrities I'd once admired were suddenly my peers. But the excitement was always overshadowed by the anxiety, desperation, and worthlessness I felt as I struggled to maintain the ultrathin figure fashion rigidly required. One time, a famous fashion editor came up to me to tell me how wonderful I looked. I thanked him to his face, but inside my head an alarm went off because I knew I hadn't eaten in two weeks.

That event, among others, led me to question my beliefs and the behavior they fueled. I realized the fashion industry was a master of illusion. Before any model steps on a fashion set, professional hair and makeup artists work for hours camouflaging her imperfections. Photographers use lighting and body positioning to manipulate the angles and shapes of the girls they photograph. Airbrushing and retouching correct any visible flaws left on the final photograph. None of it is real. I looked around me and saw that none of us could even truly live up to the standards we were setting for the rest of the world — the same standards that had caused me and so many other young people such agony. And there I was, contributing to the creation of these standards. The irony and hypocrisy of that wasn't lost on me, and I knew then that I wasn't a young woman I would admire. I was the woman I thought the rest of the world would admire. I'd never looked up to anyone for being beautiful or skinny. Strength of spirit, conviction, heart, and soul had always won my respect. I was OVER IT.

That revelation was the first step I took toward who I am now. For seven years, my body had been a battleground upon which I'd fought with myself. At twenty, I decided to fight for myself. I quit modeling in search of my "true self," beginning a journey I hope you will choose to take as well.

If you are reading *Over It*, I imagine you are taking your first step, and I hope you understand how brave you truly are. Let this book be a reminder that you aren't alone. Let it comfort you through the fear and pain you may feel at times. And let it help you become the person you would admire.

After a two-year hiatus from modeling, I returned to the business as a "plus size" model, and have found success on my own terms. Our culture has an unfortunate penchant for making people feel badly about themselves. Rather than celebrating our differences, prejudice regarding race, size, sex, sexual preference, and class is rampant. It's too hard to please everyone! Please yourself, and set yourself free.

— Kate Dillon

A Note to Parents

This book has been written for teenagers who are struggling with food or weight. If you are not sure whether or not your child has an eating disorder or needs professional help, we recommend you seek professional advice from someone who has experience working with eating disorders.

We have listed in our resource list organizations that provide free information about eating disorders, including warning signs, intervention, resources, and referrals. EDAP (Eating Disorder Awareness and Prevention, Inc.) has a toll-free line that provides national referrals at 800-931-2237.

Acknowledgments

We thank the teenagers who participated in Beyond Hunger and The Body Positive Teen Task Force. Your willingness to speak truthfully about your struggle and recovery made this book possible.

We thank all the staff at New World Library for their hard work and for believing in us and our book: Georgia Hughes for skilled editing and management of our book, and for truly caring about it from beginning to end; Mary Ann Casler for wonderful photography and art direction; Tona Pearce Myers for type design; Denise Gardner for the delightful drawings; Munro Magruder and Marjorie Conte for working hard to get our book in the hands of teens.

We thank Kate Dillon for her honesty and willingness to write such a wise and moving foreword. You will inspire many young women.

We thank the teens who were willing to model for the cover, most from the Teen Task Force: Maggie, Candace, Vanessa, Sara, Caitlin, Jordan, Kathryn, Dewan, Zarina, and Cesi.

We thank Connie Sobjack and Elizabeth Scott of The Body Positive for providing access to their wonderful and wise teen task force, for their excellent work in the prevention of eating disorders, and for their support. And thanks, Maggie Palmer, for your intelligent feedback.

We thank Patti Breitman for always believing in us and supporting us. We thank Nancy Ellis for all of her efforts on our behalf.

We thank Charlotte Lindborg for her initial editing (cleaning up the mess), and her two great teens, Dillon and Beau, for their wisdom.

We thank Jane Hirschmann and Carol Munter for pioneering this work, supporting us, inspiring us, and taking the time to write yet another great quote. And thanks to Naomi Wolf, John Gray, and Richard Carlson for supporting our work.

And last but not least, we thank the Beyond Hunger staff and board members for their excellent work, unending support, and strong commitment to this work — please keep on keeping on.

Laurelee's Acknowledgements: With love and gratitude, I thank my husband, James and my son, Clinton, for their constant support and love. A big thanks to my friends and family who continue to have the grace and caring to buy my books. I would especially like to thank Carol and the magnificent teen within her; both of them were constant and present throughout the entire process of writing this book. My last acknowledgment goes to myself and specifically to the teenage girl who lives inside of me. The truth is, it is she who always tries to keep me radical.

Carol's Acknowledgments: For his endless love, support, sacrifice, and willingness to pick up the pieces with grace and humor, I thank my husband, Jim Normandi. I could not have fulfilled this dream without you. Now it's your turn. For holding up Beyond Hunger against all odds, for keeping the vision and passion of this recovery alive, for being a wonderful partner and friend, and for the willingness to be radical, I thank Laurelee. For all of the unconditional love and support, I thank my family and my friends (you know who you are). It takes a village to write a book, and you are one incredible village. For reminding me of the unlimited wisdom we all hold within, I thank my clients. And, for reminding me of the purity of spirit, I thank Traver and Maya.

A Word from the Authors

The rite of passage from a girl to a young woman should be an experience that honors and celebrates the sacredness of feminine power, creativity, and wisdom. Unfortunately, in much of the world today, the miracle of becoming a woman is buried beneath an obsession with fat grams, calories, exercise, and scales. As a teenage girl, you get hijacked into defining your identity based on how thin you are, how good or bad you are because of what you've eaten, and how healthy you are because of how much exercise you've gotten. You are trained to ride a highway that is miles away from your true selves. Some of you will get lucky and use your eating disorder as an experience to relearn who you are. Others will die before they can even see they've been hijacked. Some will just ride that highway at a very slow pace, never quite developing an eating disorder but never quite able to love their bodies and eat peacefully, always wanting to lose that last ten pounds and wishing they hadn't eaten that piece of chocolate.

As we listen to teen after teen talk about their experiences with food and weight, and as we watch them start to get a sense of who they are beneath the desire to be thin, we wonder what would have happened to us if someone had come to our classroom and talked about eating disorders, handed us a book, or talked to us about what we were feeling. We have no doubt that these types of interventions could have had a strong impact on us. We may not have been able to stop the behaviors right away, but we would have had another truth to hold onto, like a lifeline to bring us back to what mattered.

It is our hope to bring you that lifeline.

Our goal with this book is to help you *get over it:* to find your way out from under the obsession with food and weight, and into the heart of your own truth. Both of our own eating disorders began when we were teens, and we struggled for ten to twenty years until we were able to get help. We want to help you get all of the necessary information now so you don't have to spend the next ten to twenty years struggling. It has been such an honor and blessing to witness the teenagers in our groups grapple with these issues and look in the face of their own beauty. They learn quickly because they are so close to spirit, and the wisdom that flows out of their mouths reminds us of how precious and wise our youth are.

Recovering from an eating disorder is an incredible journey. It is like going to a foreign land on a vision quest. You're not quite sure what you're looking for or even what you want, but part of you knows there is something waiting to be found. The journey is not easy. It can seem like no one speaks your language — no one understands you or your behavior. You wonder why you can't just stop throwing up, or just start eating normally. Everyone else does. It can seem like where you want to get to is so far away that it's impossible to reach, and all you can do is take baby steps each day. Sometimes it's frightening because the territory is so different from what you're used to and you have to learn new skills to get through it. And sometimes it's exciting because you discover beautiful new worlds that feed your soul.

We have outlined this vision quest for you by providing you with a map that is based on our own experience and the experience of our clients. The journey begins with reflection, asking yourself "Who am I, and where have I been? What is the story of my struggle with food and weight?" As you start to navigate the twists and turns, peaks and valleys of this journey, it becomes important to find a helpful inner guide who can lead you through the rough terrain. We define this inner guide as your compassionate voice, which needs to be strengthened in order to transform your critical voice. Now you are ready to step into this foreign land and learn everything you can about it. We ask you to become a scientific observer, bringing awareness to your feelings and behaviors in relationship to food and weight. The next challenge becomes relearning the body's basic, natural wisdom: eating when hungry, stopping when full, and eating what works for your own body. And just around the corner is the task of learning to accept your body for its own unique body type.

As you continue along your journey, you will learn to master the powerful currents of the river by acknowledging and exploring the emotions that underlie the behaviors. This will lead you to the process of unveiling your true and spiritual self, the one who has been hiding under the obsession with food and weight. As you begin to explore who you really are in this world and what you think, feel, and want, you might find yourself expressing this in ways you never imagined. Of course, at times you might feel lost, like you can't make it the rest of the way because the challenges are too great. You might be overwhelmed by all of the information you have, the feelings that are coming up, and the behaviors that aren't changing fast enough. We marked this place on the map as a volcano, but it might pop up anywhere along the journey. Here you will learn how to get through these very difficult and dark times, knowing that it is part of the healing process and you can trust yourself to get through it. Toward the end of the journey, you will gain some perspective, and be able to see others who are struggling with food and weight. We discuss ways to support others, while keeping your own recovery in place. And finally, the quest brings you the vision of who you are in truth — a radical you.

Like any other information out there, this book is laced with our own perspective. Notice what speaks to you. Notice what moves you. Notice how your own map of your own journey might be the same or different. Notice what seems true to you and what doesn't. Think critically about what we have to say and ask yourself if it is supportive and helpful. Try pieces on, and if they fit, wear them. If they don't, pass them on. You are your own best judge of your needs.

We are grateful to have lived through our eating disorders, to feel freedom from the obsession with food and weight, and for the opportunity to pass on whatever knowledge we have gained in the process. We wish the same and more for you.

Getting Over the Obsession with Food and Weight

When I was fourteen, my mother put me into modeling school. I was tall, thin, and gawky, all arms and legs. At that time the cultural ideal was round and curvy, like Marilyn Monroe, which was definitely not like me. My mother believed that going to these classes would at least help me be better poised and graceful and not such an outcast. This might have been somewhat true had not the other unforeseeable events taken place. It was the middle sixties. Suddenly Twiggy, the very first of the original "street waifs," was discovered. The pages of fashion magazines, like Vogue *or* Cosmopolitan, *started to feature extremely thin and young models like Twiggy. All of a sudden my "body type" was "in." The more knock-kneed, the more flat-chested, the taller, and the thinner, the better. At that time I weighed about 115 pounds and at five-foot eight-inches this was certainly thin. However, Twiggy weighed under a hundred pounds, so any teen model who wanted to work needed to also weigh this amount. I very much wanted to work and I very much wanted to look like Twiggy. So, I went on the first of many semi-starvation diets that I would go on throughout my life. It was in this way that I started the eating disorder that was to last well into my thirties and would*

1

many times over almost kill me. I learned many harmful lessons early on. One of the things that I learned at fourteen was that I would never really be thin enough without being very sick. I also learned that the only thing that I had going for me was the shape of my body and the way I looked. Nothing else seemed as important... not my personality, not my mind, and not my soul. I understood that my looks were my only commodity. I was constantly obsessed about food and weight. It took years and a lot of inner work to stop the obsession and raise my self-esteem high enough that I was able to appreciate my "whole" self. Little by little, I learned to love myself unconditionally no matter what and to appreciate all that I am.

— Laurelee

What's it like being constantly worried about what you look like, what you should be eating, and how much you weigh? Well, chances are, if you live in the United States and you are female, you know exactly what it's like. The truth is that 65 percent of eleven-year-old girls worry that they are too fat; 80 percent of eleven-year-old girls report they are dieting[1]; 90 percent of high school junior and senior adolescents diet regularly.[2] Chances are that by the time you are a junior in high school, you are already worrying about your weight and what you eat.

Most likely you know someone who is always on a diet, who is scared of getting fat, or who has an eating disorder. You probably hear, "I'm too fat," or "I shouldn't have eaten that," or "I can't eat that," or "I have to lose some weight," over and over again. And most likely, it's not your male friends that are saying these things. It's a female thing. Ninety percent of people with eating disorders are female.[3] It's also a young-adult thing. One-third of eating disorder victims reported that their eating problems started between ages eleven and fifteen, and 86 percent of eating disorder victims reported that their eating problems started by age twenty.[4] But why is this? Why are *young females* dying to be thin? Why are *young females* throwing up, taking laxatives, swallowing diet pills, starving themselves, and hating their bodies?

The desire to be thin, disliking our bodies, dieting, starving, overeating, taking diet pills or laxatives, excessive exercising, and worrying about becoming fat are all *symptoms* of an eating disorder. They are *not the cause* of the eating disorder. The causes of the obsession with food and weight are very complex and different for everyone. They can include the following:

Growing up in a culture and/or family that encourages dieting and teaches females to dislike their natural feminine bodies

Everywhere I turned I got the message I was too fat. My brother was always teasing me and my friends, calling us fat. My mother was always on some diet and used to say over and over again how her thighs were too big. Since I'm built like her, that meant mine were too. You just sort of learn by hearing comments that everyone makes about what's okay and what's not. My friends were always trying to make sure they didn't gain weight. And I could see in every magazine model, in every female movie star, and in every Barbie doll what I was supposed to look like.

— Ariel

As females in this culture, we learn at a young age what we are *supposed* to look like and act like. We are supposed to look and act like the models in *Seventeen* and *Cosmopolitan,* and yet most of us are not born with bodies that will ever look like those bodies. No matter how hard we try, we can't make one body type into another.

To be female in this culture is to be on a diet, worried about weight, or on the verge of an eating disorder. To be female is to hate our bodies and to strive for an ideal body that is unnatural for most of us. The message that females should dislike their natural feminine body is everywhere. Think about it. Billions of dollars every year are spent on advertising showing very thin models. And billions more are spent by the rest of us on diet programs so we can look like all these models. We are actually taught to diet and hate our bodies by hearing negative messages and unrealistic standards over and over again through advertisements, magazines, television, movies, our own friends, and sometimes our own families. It is everywhere. It is a cultural attitude.

Not knowing how to deal with overwhelming feelings and using eating-disordered behaviors to cope with them

By the time I was thirteen years old, I had already learned that my body was too fat and that I should be dieting. When my body started changing from a preteen body into a rounder, curvier, sexually developed woman's body, I thought I was getting too fat. I believed that my body should be like the ones I saw in the magazines: tall and thin. Since my body wasn't like that, I believed it was wrong. I had a lot of feelings of insecurity as a teenager about who I was, about relationships with other people, and about my sexuality. But I didn't really know how to deal with these feelings. I put myself on a diet because I thought if I lost weight it would fix everything. Now I can see that what I really needed was some reassurance, some help with my self-esteem, and some way to cope with the overwhelming feelings. But the only way I knew how to make myself feel better was to eat. And the only way I knew how to be accepted was to diet and lose weight. I got into the cycle of eating to make myself feel better, and then dieting because I ate so much. As time went on, this became worse, and I began throwing up so I wouldn't gain any more weight. By the time I was in college, I was a severe bulimic. The part of me that needed to be loved, comforted, and reassured got buried beneath the bingeing, purging, and obsession with food and weight.

— Carol

We all experience a variety of feelings in our lives, yet many of us are not taught how to understand them, express them, and process them in a way that is constructive. So we try to find any way we can to take care of ourselves. For some, overeating can soothe or numb uncomfortable feelings. For others, undereating can do the same by creating a false sense of strength, control, and worthiness. Sometimes the constant thinking about our food and weight keeps us from experiencing our feelings. Although these behaviors start as a way to cope, they end up hurting us more than helping us.

Defining who we are by what we look like or what we do creates insecurity and low self-esteem

At twelve, I was hospitalized three times for anorexia. Sometimes I was fed intravenously, and I was always monitored to make sure that I didn't throw up. I thought I'd be prettier and happier if I starved myself. I thought anorexia was the only thing I had going for me. My recovery was a long, slow process. But I realized that the root cause of my anorexia was self-hatred, and insecurity about who I was. I began to question, "Why should anyone be measured by how much she weighs?"

— Vanessa

When we are taught that our value as a person is based on our accomplishments or beauty, instead of who we are as spiritual beings, our self-esteem becomes based on achieving these goals. We think we are good if we are thin and bad if we are fat. We think we are worthy if we get straight A's in school, and worthless if we get straight C's. We push ourselves to meet other people's standards because we want to please them, not because we are pursuing our own unique gifts and strengths. The experience of becoming a woman and developing sexually is laced with expectations of eating certain foods and looking a certain way. So our identity as women becomes focused around "Am I fat or thin? Am I eating non-fattening foods or not? Am I the right weight or the wrong weight?" With all of the incredible things women can and are doing today, do you know what most women want to be? Thin!

Our identity, self-esteem, and security have become so tied to food and weight that we have forgotten the potential of who we really are. And the problem is that if we can't be as *thin* as we think we *should* be, or as *beautiful* as we think we *should* be, or as *whatever it is* that we think we *should* be, we feel bad about ourselves. Feeling bad about ourselves (low self-esteem) creates the even more desperate need to be whatever we think we should be (thin) and puts pressure on us. These pressures and uncomfortable feelings can actually cause us to overeat, undereat, and obsess even more, leading us into a vicious cycle.

A way to protect ourselves from physical, sexual, or emotional abuse, or other trauma

I remember realizing one day that I no longer got comments about my body. On one hand this was upsetting to me because I hated my body and thought that everyone saw me as fat and ugly. But on the other hand I felt safer because I didn't have to deal with men saying, "Nice tits," or "Check out her healthy chest," or grabbing my butt and breasts. It dawned on me that maybe having some weight on me protected me in a way that I didn't otherwise know how to.

— Carol

Sometimes changing our bodies, such as gaining or losing weight, can be a way of protecting our bodies from being treated as sexual objects. Like Carol, we may feel that if we are very fat, or very thin, we will no longer be sexually attractive and will be safe from further harassment. This is also true of more severe trauma, such as physical or sexual abuse.

Also, if we have a traumatic experience in our lives, we have to find ways to survive the emotional pain. As a child, one of the most available ways of coping with the pain is using food to soothe oneself. As we said before, overeating, undereating, and/or obsessing can be a way to manage overwhelming feelings.

So, as you see, the behaviors of the eating disorders are just *symptoms* that are a response to other underlying pressures. In other words, when we worry about what we look like, we are really worrying about whether or not we will be liked. When we worry about how fat our thighs are, we're really afraid that we are "unacceptable." When we are eating a lot of food when we're not hungry, we may be anxious or angry or unhappy and the food helps to calm us down. When we are refusing to eat when we're hungry, we may be trying to punish or hurt ourselves, or trying to feel safe by taking charge of one of the few things we have control over. When we look in the mirror and say, "Yuck," we are just repeating what we have learned by listening to our mothers, friends, relatives, or the media.

You probably already know about each eating disorder, having heard it from your parents, your teachers, and even your friends. You've read about it in magazines and seen stories about it on television. We know this information can be very confusing. Some of you may not have a typical eating disorder, but instead find yourself having fat thoughts, hating your body, or worrying about what you eat. If this is the case, this book can still help you find the tools to accept your body and have a healthy relationship with food. This in turn will prevent you from developing an eating disorder. So, here are simple descriptions of each of the three main eating disorders and some quotes from young people who have been there.

WHAT IS COMPULSIVE EATING?

I can remember at twelve years old being alone at home in the afternoons because both my parents worked. I would get very bored and lonely and sometimes scared. To feel better I would sit on the couch, turn on the TV, and eat whatever I could find. I would eat and eat and eat until I felt better. I began to worry that I was gaining weight so I put myself on a diet. I would try not to eat too much at school, but when I got home the only way I could get through the lonely afternoon was to eat. The more I ate, the more I hated myself, and I would put myself right back onto another diet. I could never stick to the diet because eating was the only way I could get through the day.

— Amber

Amber learned to cope with her lonely afternoons by eating to soothe herself. It didn't matter whether she was hungry or full. Her need to take care of herself emotionally overruled her physical needs. Compulsive eating (also called binge eating) is an attempt to take care of oneself with food. For Amber, it was a way to make herself feel better, at least temporarily. A compulsive eater becomes out of touch with her body's messages that signal hunger and fullness, and she starts overeating to help herself cope with uncomfortable feelings she is holding inside. This may lead to binge eating (eating large amounts of food at a time) in order to keep those feelings from surfacing.

We also view compulsive eating as a response to restrictive dieting, which can lead to increased food intake and binge eating. Feeling bad about your body size can also lead to dieting and compulsive eating. A compulsive eater often worries about what she can and can't eat, and how much she should and shouldn't weigh. Sometimes these thoughts become so loud and frequent that they drown out real feelings.

Compulsive eating can result in weight gain. However, that may or may not cause physical harm to your body. There are many myths about the relationship between weight gain and physical health. If you have concerns about weight gain, it is best to consult a doctor who understands compulsive eating, the negative effects of dieting, and the myths regarding weight gain and its impact on physical health. For resources and referrals, see the resource list at the back of the book.

What Is Bulimia Nervosa?

Last summer my friend and I read about a girl who threw up after she ate a lot. We thought this was a great idea, so we started doing it ourselves. We would go over to her house after swimming and eat cookies, cakes, and chips until we were so full. And then we would make ourselves throw up. We did this all summer long, we called it "our secret diet aid." I thought my stomach was too flabby and doing this made me feel like my stomach was really flat. But it also made my stomach really hurt. And now I am scared because I am so out of control. I want to stop, but I can't.

— Heidi

This is a classic case of something too good to be true. Heidi thought she found a solution to her overeating and her "flabby" stomach. But, once she started purging, she couldn't stop. The reality is, this kind of "diet aid" not only doesn't work, but it is also dangerous and can be deadly.

Bulimia nervosa is a form of compulsive eating where you binge and then do some kind of purging. Types of purging may include vomiting, fasting, excessive exercise, or use of diuretics, laxatives, or diet pills. Many young women start purging after they feel they've failed at dieting. They either feel they were eating too much, or their body was too fat, or both. Like compulsive eaters, people with bulimia usually spend a lot of time being concerned with their food and their weight. They might also tend to have difficulty experiencing and resolving overwhelming feelings.

Bulimia can be harmful to your body. It can cause digestive problems, dental problems, diabetes, damage to the esophagus, and electrolyte and chemical imbalances that can lead to irregular heartbeats, heart failure, and death.

What Is Anorexia Nervosa?

Last year I was going with a guy who was always telling me that I was fat because I didn't look like a model. After he broke up with me I was too upset to eat. I lost some weight and I really got a lot of attention because of it. All my girlfriends were so jealous of me. So I started to see how little I could eat. Every day I tried to eat less than the day before. I just got thinner and thinner. But, in a weird way, I felt really strong and powerful. My old boyfriend wouldn't say I was too fat, now. The bad thing is that these days all I can think about is how much thinner I could get and not die.

— Les

Unfortunately many girls, in order to look like a supermodel, need to develop an eating disorder. This is exactly what is happening with Les. If she does not stop her drive to be ever thinner, she may endanger her life. In her quest for a different body, Les may kill herself.

Anorexia nervosa is self-starvation. People with anorexia refuse to maintain their body weight over a minimal natural weight for their age and height. These young women often have a distorted image of their bodies. People with anorexia who are very thin can look into the mirror and see their bodies as very fat. They have an obsessive fear of gaining weight or becoming fat even though they are underweight. Many times they have a very negative and critical voice inside their heads that tells them over and over again how fat they are. They spend an enormous amount of time thinking about controlling their food and weight or they indulge in excessive exercising.

More deaths are directly caused by anorexia than the other eating disorders. Anorexia can cause loss of menstrual periods, loss of ability to have children, osteoporosis, congestive heart failure, irregular heart rhythm, and damage to kidneys, brain, and digestive system.

These are just a very few examples of girls who have had eating disorders. Often individuals will have more than one type of eating disorder and will bounce back and forth among all three — compulsive eating, bulimia, and anorexia.

Remember that everyone is different and will have different ways they struggle with food and weight, as well as different reasons why they have this struggle. What is important is to understand your own unique way and to get the right help. Eating disorders are curable and by working with them you can bring yourself back into living a joyful, fulfilling, and healthy life.

THE STRUGGLE TO BE OURSELVES

*All I ever thought about was what I was going to eat that day,
how much I weighed, and how I looked in my clothes. I was sure
everyone was looking at me thinking, "She sure is fat." I kept my
grades up and I kept my friends, but I really wasn't that interested in either. In fact, I even lost interest in myself. It's like, I
just sort of forgot who I was.*

— Tanya

Obsessing about food and weight makes it hard to be who you
really are. Young adulthood is a time to explore who you are as a
person. It's a time to discover who you are in relationship to your
family, girlfriends, boyfriends, and community. It's a time to find
out what special gifts and talents you have that make you different from everyone else. It's a time to dream about what you want
to do with your life. It's a time to explore your feelings, your sexuality, and your physical and spiritual self. But let's face it ... who
has time for all this when all you can think about is fitting into
that pair of jeans, not eating too much fat, or wishing you looked
like that model on the cover of some fashion magazine?

We know what it's like to waste all those years worrying about
food and fat. We've been there and, to tell you the truth, it stinks.
It is frightening to think that because our culture is obsessed with
dieting and having a "perfect" body, we also learn to be obsessed.
This obsession is dangerous. It can be a matter of life and death.

In order to stop worrying about how fat you are or how many
fat grams you should eat, we believe that you have to try to find
out who you really are underneath your obsession with food and
weight. That's what this book is about: finding your true self. To
do this, it's important to first become aware of your own unique
eating patterns. Then it's about discovering the wisdom and

unique beauty of your own body. It's important to start listening to your feelings and learning how to express them without eating too much or too little. It's time to explore what your passions, talents, and gifts are. Through this process you learn who you really are, not who you think you should be. You will find that underneath this constant struggle with food and weight, buried beneath your own insecurity and symptoms, there is a part of you crying out to be seen and heard, a part of you that is precious, wise, and different from everyone else.

Your Challenge

I look at my stomach and say, "Why can't I be thin? Why can't my body be okay?" That's all I want.

— Sarah

As you read this book, keep in mind that you have received a lot of very negative information about your size, your body, your rights as a female, and your very self. Most of this has come from the society you have been born into. It takes an incredible amount of courage, strength, and tenacity not to give in to the hundreds of hurtful pressures that are put on you and on your female body. In the support groups at Beyond Hunger, our nonprofit organization, we call this "swimming against the tide." You will often feel that you are swimming upstream against a steady barrage of messages to keep you always wanting something other than what you have. We, adults and teens alike, have fallen over and over again for the promise of how good life will be when we are thinner, smaller, taller, different, sexier, better. In order to recover from an eating disorder and a horrible body image you must learn how to love and understand yourself no matter what. It will also take a lot of nerve and commitment to take a stand against the mainstream culture. *This is your challenge.* Only now are we, as adults, beginning to understand what messages we have been passing down to our girls about food and weight. It's time to stop the cycle once and for all. But it's up to you because you are the next generation. You can do it. You will discover how by listening to your own inner truth.

Notes

[1] Mellin, L. M., C. E. Irwin, Jr., and S. Scully. "Disordered Eating Characteristics in Girls: A Survey of Middle Class Children." *Journal of the American Dietetic Association,* vol. 92, 1992, pp. 851–53.

[2] Council on Size and Weight Discrimination.

[3] EDAP — Eating Disorder Awareness and Prevention.

[4] ANAD — National Association of Anorexia Nervosa and Associated Disorders.

Telling Your Story

Everyone Has a Story — What's Yours?

I'll never forget the first time I talked about my eating disorder from beginning to end. My heart was pounding, my palms were sweating, and I had visions of people's mouths dropping open in horror, terrified of the ugly truths that were tumbling out of my very own mouth. But once I started, I couldn't stop. Even though I was terrified people would think I was crazy, the need to finally voice the truth of my secret life took over. I was pretty sure that I was in a safe place with trusted people, so I took the risk. It was as if the cork in the bottle had been pierced, and the memories that I had neatly tucked away dripped out, one by one. I talked about things that I was ashamed of — about eating a whole frozen cake, about throwing up six times in one day, and about hating my body. And the amazing thing was that no one ran screaming out of the room. In fact, they were very moved by what I had to say. Of course, all the way home I worried about what I said and how stupid it was, but that didn't matter because I knew that somehow I was different. For the first time I really listened to myself, my truth, and my own story.

— Carol

Each one of us is unique, with different families, pasts, feelings, dreams, and problems. Even though we may have similar struggles with food and weight, we each have a different story about how those struggles started and how they grew. Telling your *own* story about your struggle with food and weight will empower you with new understandings about your own unique problems. In this way you can then take steps to change. This is why we tell our stories.

As you tell your own story, you might learn many new things about yourself, such as what you think and feel about yourself and others, and what you feel about experiences you've had in the past. Some of these things you've never told anyone else, and maybe some of them you haven't even told yourself. Other things may be uncomfortable to look at, and some may be hard to understand. Go at your own pace, exploring what you're comfortable with. You might find that your story will start out one way, but will change as you learn more about your own strengths, insights, and ways of looking at the world.

Here is an exercise to help you tell your own story. You don't *have* to do this or any other exercises in this book. We've just found that they have been very helpful to those who have tried them.

TRY THIS: Telling Your Story

Get a pen and paper and find a quiet, safe place where you can sit down and write. We've given you some questions below as guidelines to help you get started, but feel free just to write whatever comes to mind. Don't worry about grammar or spelling or what it sounds like. Don't worry about what other people will think about it. You are free to throw your writing away when you're done if you want to. However if you're comfortable with keeping it, you might want to start a binder or a journal of this work so you can look back on it later.

1. Start by trying to remember the first time you felt bad about your body or about food. How old were you? Was it a specific event or just a general time period?

2. How did this change over the years? Was there anything specific you remember that made it better or worse?

3. How did your family, friends, teachers, and other people in your life influence how you felt about your body or food?

4. What is your first memory of either overeating or undereating when you were feeling emotional (eating or controlling your food when lonely, afraid, or angry)? How old were you? Who was with you? What were you feeling? What were you wanting?

5. How do you think having this struggle with food and weight has affected you in the past, and how does it affect you now?

6. How have you tried to deal with this struggle?

7. What do you really want to happen with your food and body?

8. What do you really want to happen with your life?

9. What do you think you need right now?

You are doing this just for yourself, so be as truthful to yourself as possible. Remember to tell not only the bad parts but also the good parts. The point is to let yourself in on all of your experiences, the "real" ones, as well as your inner thoughts, wishes, desires, dreams, fears, embarrassments — all of it.

Spend as much time as you need to tell your own story to yourself. Do not try to rush through this process. You are meeting a very special person who has had many amazing and challenging things happen to her. You are meeting you.

FINDING COMPASSION FOR YOUR STORY

One day I was sitting in group listening to this girl talk, and I felt so touched by what she was saying. She was talking about how much pressure she felt to be in good shape from her family and her swim coach. It wasn't that they were telling her this, it's just sort of a legacy from her brothers and sisters that she felt she had to live up to. She was getting so down on herself for not being able to lose weight, and not being able to be like them, and I found myself getting so angry that she had to go through this. I wanted to tell her that she was beautiful and perfect, and she didn't need to prove herself to anyone. Then, I began to realize that her story was similar to mine, which is why I was so moved by it. And what I wanted to tell her I also needed to tell myself. Believe me, it was a lot harder to say to myself.

— Jasmine

Sometimes it's much easier to feel compassion and kindness for our friends than for ourselves. We might try to find the right words to make a friend feel better but we don't even think of trying to do that for ourselves. Many people who struggle with food and weight believe that there is something terribly wrong with them — that they are the problem. So what happens is that they become very frustrated and critical of themselves, wishing they were thinner, prettier, smarter, or wishing they wouldn't eat so much, or so little, or throw up, or whatever. They think, "How come I can't stop eating? How come I have no willpower? How come I'm so weak and stupid? How come I can't eat like a normal person? How come I know I'm killing myself but I can't stop starving myself? What's wrong with me? Why am I so stupid, lazy, ugly, crazy, out of control, bad, or wrong?"

We don't believe that people have eating disorders for any of those reasons. As we've said before, we believe people have eating disorders because 1) they have grown up in a culture that teaches females to diet and dislike their bodies, 2) they don't know how to process and understand overwhelming feelings, 3) they are insecure about who they are as people, or 4) they are protecting themselves in response to past trauma. We have heard story after story of women and girls who develop eating disorders in order to cope with very difficult situations in their lives. Their eating disorders have helped them to survive.

I remember the first day I binged. My boyfriend had told me that he wanted to break up with me. When I asked him why, he said that he just felt bored and he wasn't attracted to me anymore. I walked away, holding back my tears, vowing that no one would see me cry. I was so confused. I didn't understand why. I started thinking maybe I was boring, maybe I was unattractive, maybe I was too fat. I thought of ways I could become more exciting, more beautiful, more thin. I decided I'd go an a diet. I walked home, praying that no one would be there. As soon as I got through the front door, I headed toward the refrigerator. I ate everything I could get my hands on. I ate until I was so sick I couldn't eat anymore. But at least I didn't feel that horrible pit in my stomach anymore.

— Madelyn

Usually when we overeat, undereat, or worry about our food or weight, there is a reason. For Madelyn, she began to think she was unattractive. Even though that's not what her boyfriend said (he said *he* wasn't attracted to her anymore), that's how she heard it because she felt bad about being rejected and that there must be something wrong with her. So in her own mind *she* decided she was unattractive, too fat, and needed to be on a diet. She was overwhelmed with feelings of sadness, anger, and confusion. She did not want anyone to see her cry so she just held all of her feelings in. When she got to her house, instead of knowing how to take care of herself in another way (such as letting herself cry or calling a friend), she just kept eating and eating until she began to calm down.

Madelyn is not bad or stupid or wrong because she ate. In fact, she was trying to take care of herself in the only way she knew how. If she had known other ways to take care of herself she would have used them. And this is true for everyone with eating disorders. You are not wrong or bad or stupid because you use food to feel better. You are just trying to cope with the challenges of your life in the best way you know how. In order to learn ways to cope that don't hurt you (because eating disorders not only hurt you but can kill you), it's important to understand how your struggle with food and weight has helped you to survive.

Your eating disorder started out from a place of strength, not weakness. It is a part of you that was trying to help you survive. In order to heal, it helps to understand how this struggle was trying to take care of you and to have compassion for your eating disorder, your story, and your self.

The following exercise can help you find the reasons why you started struggling with food and weight issues and to help you develop compassion for yourself.

TRY THIS: Finding Compassion

Go back over the story you wrote in the first exercise. Ask yourself these questions and, if you'd like, write down the answers.

1. How did you learn to dislike your body?
2. What might have been some reasons for your over- or undereating?
3. How has your eating disorder helped you to cope with difficult situations in your life?
4. How has dieting made you feel better or worse about yourself?
5. Do you judge your struggle with food and weight as good or bad?
6. How do you think your eating disorder has tried to help you?
7. If your eating disorder could talk, what would it say?

Now pretend that the story is a friend's story. Read it again and listen with a sense of interest, caring concern, and compassion. As you do this, think about the kinds of supportive and caring things you would tell your friend. Can you say these things to yourself? Try. It might be hard at first, or even feel silly, but keep trying.

WHO'S THAT CRITIC IN YOUR BRAIN?

Sometimes I think I'm driving myself crazy. No matter what's going on or where I am, a million times a day, I tell myself how fat and totally gross I look. I could be walking down the street and see myself in the window and I think, "Oh my God, I look so fat!" Or I may be at a party and I catch a glimpse of myself in the mirror and I think, "I can't believe how big my stomach is." I am so sick of always telling myself how fat and ugly I am.

— Amee

Amee is the perfect example of someone who has taken the critical voices of the world into her mind and is now using them against herself and her body. She has learned this behavior; it is a learned behavior, not her natural instinct. Just as she learned to tie her shoes, she learned how to speak to herself in this way. At some point, Amee was told that she was fat, and that she was gross. Maybe not in those exact words but somewhere along the line, as she was growing up, she was exposed to negative messages. At home, at school, from her peers, and through the media, she has gotten the idea that she is not okay as she is.

As a female in our society, she was raised with the messages that she was too fat, too tall, too flat, too big, too wrong. Believing these messages, she began to tell them to herself. She took our culture's fear of fat and hatred for the natural feminine body and turned it into her own fear and hatred. Whatever positive inner voices she may have had at one time have been buried under this hatred and fear.

This is what makes it really hard for the person who has an eating disorder. She has learned to blame all her problems on her body instead of trying to figure out what is truly bothering her. No matter what comes up for her — whether it's school, friends, family, or work — she puts the blame onto her body, which is also putting the blame onto her *self*. She cannot see her problems as being separate from who she is. She loses her perspective: *Who* she is and *how* she is have become the reason for her problems.

Instead of having a problem, she thinks she is the problem. She no longer comes up with reasonable or workable solutions to her problems. Instead, she goes immediately to self-doubt and decides that who she is and how she is must change in order to fix what is wrong. The voice inside her that puts her down and tells her that she is the problem is called her "inner critic."

We all have inner critics. They are a necessary part of us. When we learn how to work with our inner critic instead of letting it control us, it can be a positive force within ourselves. We can use it to let us know when changes need to be made. We can use it to warn us of danger. We can use it to tell us right from wrong. But first, we need to turn the negative messages into helpful, loving, positive ones.

How do we turn the negative into the positive? The first step is to tune in and identify these critical voices. We then need to learn to question the critical voice and understand what we are really trying to tell ourselves. Know that you were not born telling yourself how fat and gross you are. When you were a baby you were delighted with yourself, just as all babies are. Imagine letting yourself go back to that same sense of wonder, joy, and self-love.

MAKING PEACE WITH YOUR CRITIC

My mom is always on a diet and there are diet reminders all over the fridge. The biggest one is a big, pink pig with a "don't pig out" saying on it. Every time I try to eat something, I see that big, pink pig and tell myself to not "pig out." Even if I'm hungry and all I'm gonna eat is a sandwich or something, I still see that pig. And then if I do eat, I think that I am a big, pink pig.

— Clarissa

In order to make peace with the critical voice that's inside our heads, it is necessary to become our own nonjudgmental observer. This means learning how to observe and listen to yourself without the shaming messages you have learned.

For Clarissa, she had to learn to understand that just the image of the pig was enough to make her stop eating altogether. Because she had been told she was a "chubby" child and because her mother was always complaining and worried about her own weight as well as Clarissa's, she was very afraid of becoming a "pig." As time went on she got more and more scared of being fat. Finally she became afraid of eating altogether. She almost had to be hospitalized for anorexia. This really woke up everyone in her family.

She worked hard to become aware of the shameful messages she had learned. She stopped using the well-meaning diet slogans as critical messages and came up with positive statements about herself instead.

Learning how to observe ourselves without shame or criticism is one of the most powerful things we can do for ourselves. We call this becoming your own science project. Just as in biology or chemistry, the scientist learns to stand back and observe whatever is going on with an open mind. If she mixes formula A and B and she gets nothing but a huge mess, she doesn't get mad and criticize the formula for behaving this way. Instead, she says, "Isn't that interesting. I wonder what makes A and B react this way?" We learn from science that we can develop a part of ourselves to observe and question our behaviors with a sense of detachment and curiosity. When we can do this, for even a few moments, we gain a special power to change the things about ourselves that we've chosen to change.

So, whether you are working on figuring out why you are obsessing about your food or your weight, or you just want to understand something about yourself, it's a lot more productive and kind to say to yourself, "Isn't this interesting?!"

TRY THIS: Making Peace with Your Critic

1. Be aware of your own criticisms about your body. Ask yourself where these judgments come from. From your parents? Teachers? Friends? Culture? The refrigerator door? Is this what *you* really think about yourself and your body? Or is this what you have been told? Can you figure out what other messages might be underneath the judgmental messages?

2. Notice how many times a day you mentally scream at yourself, especially about your appearance and how you eat. How often do you compare yourself with others and find that you come up lacking? Does doing this make you feel better or worse about yourself? Who else in your life screams at themselves in this way? A parent? Your friends? Are they happy or at peace with themselves? Observe babies or small children and notice how much they enjoy their own bodies. Can you remember when you felt this way about yourself?

3. When you find yourself judging yourself, stop a moment and try to create a more open, nonjudgmental way of treating yourself. Imagine yourself having the ability to just wonder with interest what it is that you are doing or thinking. This voice may say things like "Hmm, I wonder if I'm hungry for lunch?" instead of "What is wrong with me? I'm such a fat pig for being hungry again!" Or "Oh, this is what I look like today," instead of "I can't believe how fat and disgusting I look in these jeans." Or "Isn't this interesting, I just had a fight with my boyfriend and now I'm overeating." This seems really stupid at first, but soon your nonjudgmental voice will become more familiar to you and easier to hear.

REACHING OUT

One day at gym class I started to feel faint. I had been either not eating, or throwing up after eating, for a couple of months. I hadn't eaten all day and I had vomited the last thing I ate before I went to bed the night before. I got really scared and started crying. My best friend saw me and went with me to tell our coach. My coach talked to me and calmed me down and made me promise to tell my mom. I was really worried that my mom was going to be mad at me, but she hugged me and told me she would get me help.

— Suzie

As you gain more knowledge about yourself, it is extremely important to tell your story to someone else. This is "coming out of the closet" time. The main reason for this is to get support so you don't have to be isolated and alone.

Look around until you find a trusted friend or relative to whom you can tell your story. This may be a teacher, a parent, a spiritual advisor, a best friend, a counselor, or a loving aunt. Whoever it may be, make sure that it is someone who will honor you for who you are, not for what you look like. Discuss what you have been going through with your eating disorder and how you are now changing. Let them know what it has been like for you to eat too much or to eat too little. Let them know what it's been like to hate your body and yourself, to carry the burden of blame for your life upon your young shoulders.

Also, this trusted friend or relative needs to know how to support you in the changes you are making. Let them know what they can do to support you. Be aware that sometimes friends and family may not be able to completely understand. If they haven't had the disorder or a similar struggle, they may not be able to get why you can't just start eating, or stop throwing up, or whatever. With best intentions, they may try to give you advice or ask you questions you find embarrassing or even insulting. That's okay. Don't take it personally. Eating disorders are complex and many people don't understand them or know how to support people with them. If you feel comfortable enough, you can give them resources to help educate themselves.

There are many other types of support for you as you go through this process, which we will discuss at the end of this book. But, for now, just let yourself realize that you no longer have to do this alone.

This recovery is about being aware and truthful, to yourself and to others. Trust yourself and let yourself know that the truth really will set you free.

To Be Aware

Finding Out Who You Are and What You Need

My family and friends started making comments about me being too thin, and I would assure them I was eating. I didn't want them to know what I was doing because I didn't want to stop and I didn't want to worry them. Plus I felt stupid about it. It seemed like I should be able to start eating more, but I just couldn't. I started eating just to get my parents off my back, and then I went running to get the food out of me. There were so many voices telling me what to do, but the only voice I could hear was the one that said I was too fat. I didn't even know what I thought or felt anymore . . . there was no room to know . . . it was too scary to know. I felt alone, like no one understood because if they did they would just leave me alone. Then I had to go get treatment, and I remember being really scared because I knew I had to start dealing with what I was doing. It took me a while to be able to talk about it, and then slowly I was able to be aware of what I was doing and under-stand why I was doing it.

— Lilly

You are a unique individual. You are different from everyone else in the universe. Your struggles with food and weight are also unique to you. There may be some things you are doing, thinking, or even feeling that are the same as other people do, think, or feel, but most likely your actions, thoughts, and feelings will be expressed in your own style. Because of this, no one else can know exactly what you are going through and what you need. No one else can truly help you unless you are able and willing to start understanding yourself.

Remember, you have valuable wisdom inside of you that only you can hear. Parents, friends, counselors, or others may be able to help you learn to listen, but only you can hear it. Only you know what you do when you're alone, what you feel in your body, and what thoughts you have in your head. You hold the key to your own recovery, but it may take a while to discover what it's buried under.

To begin understanding yourself, observe and become aware of what is going on between you and food and your weight. By becoming aware, you begin to gather information about yourself. This information helps you pinpoint who you are and what you need. But gathering this information can also be scary and overwhelming. People feel a lot of shame when they have struggles with food and weight. Sometimes the shame is about the eating behaviors themselves, like overeating, undereating, bingeing, purging, taking pills or laxatives, or whatever you're doing. Sometimes the shame is about your own body type. Sometimes the shame is that you think you shouldn't be doing what you're doing but you can't stop, so you feel like something's wrong with you. You wonder how you could let your parents down, or your girlfriends/boyfriends, or yourself. Sometimes something has happened in your past that you feel ashamed about. These feelings of shame can be very uncomfortable, so uncomfortable that sometimes it's just easier to go into denial, to not want to be truthful about what you are doing because the truth is too painful to look at.

As you begin to notice your own patterns surrounding food and weight, remember to have compassion for yourself, to stop judging yourself, and to find your noncritical, nurturing voice. Every time you become aware of something new about yourself and you discover you are being critical of yourself, you may have to go back and read chapter two again, until you can find compassion for yourself.

When my therapist first talked to me about recovering from my eating disorder, part of me just wanted to run out the door. I didn't want to start eating. I didn't want to give up throwing up. I was afraid I would gain one hundred pounds in a week. I didn't want to give up my power over my food and my body. I knew that everyone wanted me to get better and that I "should" stop what I was doing. And even though somewhere I knew my behavior was hurting me, I was scared that I couldn't live without it.

— Laurelee

It may also be difficult to become aware of what you are doing because you are afraid that if you acknowledge your behaviors, your eating disorder, you may have to stop them, and that is scary. The rituals surrounding your struggles with food and weight have become important to you. They have become a way to help you survive and feel better about yourself. Sometimes you don't want to give up dieting, or exercising, or purging, even if it is killing you. And you know what? That is understandable. How can you give up something that is a way of survival when you haven't learned any other way to survive yet? So for right now, we're not asking you to give anything up. We're just asking you to begin to become conscious of what is going on with you so you can figure out what it is you really need that you are not getting. Then you can find new ways to take care of yourself. With new ways to take care of yourself, you will find it much easier and less scary to give up the old ways that are helping you cope, but hurting your body.

LISTENING TO YOURSELF

When I get home from school, I'm starving. But because I'm always on a diet, I don't let myself eat anything. I make myself wait until my mom gets home and cooks dinner. But then once dinner is over I just eat and eat until time to go to bed. Everybody in my family yells at me about this but not as loud as I yell at myself. I think if I ate when I got home maybe I wouldn't eat so much after dinner, but I'm too scared. Plus I'm too fat to eat anyway.

— Melissa

Melissa has put herself in a hard place. She doesn't feel she can eat when she's hungry (after school) and she doesn't have any trust that she will stop eating (after dinner). Somewhere along the line she has stopped listening to her body, especially about food and eating. For her, the trick will be to become aware of her hunger and to watch what she does with it.

We all have eating patterns that we've developed over the years. Some of the patterns help us and some do us no good at all. Some we've learned from our family, some from our teachers, some from our friends, and some from the culture in which we live.

The time has come to start to listen to yourself and understand what will be best for you and your own unique body. This is a conscious and thoughtful process. It takes becoming an observant person instead of a critical person. You need to practice just noticing, without yelling at yourself, what you are doing around food and your body. An observer will see what is going on and be okay with it; a critic will see what is going on and start yelling about it. It's a lot easier to come to terms with a behavior you might want to change when you are not mad at yourself for doing the behavior.

For instance, Melissa knows that she is hungry when she gets home from school, but she won't let herself eat because she thinks she's too fat and she's scared that once she starts eating she will never stop. Of course, she proves to herself this is true because she eats and eats after dinner is over. What would happen if she ate when she was hungry? Would she need to overeat later? We don't know and neither will Melissa until she observes what her behaviors and patterns are around food and eating, understands why she does what she does, and then tries something different.

For now, the thing to do is just to notice your behavior patterns. We all do things all the time that we don't even think about. We get up in the mornings, get dressed, leave the house, come home again, put on our pj's, and go to sleep, with lots and lots of stuff in between. At this stage we're asking you to be super aware of all of these different things. This is so that later on you can make decisions about whether you are making choices that are in line with what you really want to do, especially with your choices around your food or your body. Don't try to do anything different right now. Just pay attention to your habits. And no yelling.

TRY THIS: Observing Your Eating Patterns

Ask yourself three different things often throughout the day:

1. *When do I eat?* Dinner time? After school? In the mornings? Late at night? You might be hungry right after school. Sometimes you might only be hungry

when you wake up in the morning, then again at lunch, and then again at dinnertime. Lots of people eat every few hours, and even more people eat at all different times each and every day. There is no "right way" and there is no "wrong way." What you are trying to see is "your way."

2. *How do I eat?* With others? Only when I'm alone? Fast? Slowly? We knew a girl named Ashley who used to only eat when she was completely alone. She also ate very fast and didn't stop until the food was all gone. When she really looked at this behavior, she realized that she was so disgusted with herself because she was convinced that it was "gross" to eat, that she judged herself harshly each time she got hungry. She would only allow herself to eat when no one could see her and then be done as soon as possible, so she could stop being "grossed out." It was hard for her to not want to change this behavior once she really saw it, but it was important to stay with it because of the lesson she was learning.

3. *Where do I eat?* Only at home? Only at school? Only at Grandma's? Another girl, Ami, only wanted to eat at home. She would turn down food everywhere but at home. For her the issue was safety. She felt that people judged her for her weight so she only felt safe at home in her own kitchen. She lived with her grandmother who loved to cook for her, and her grandmother had made it okay for her to eat there. Later on, she got to work on making it okay to eat anywhere, but at first she just needed to see what she was doing around eating times.

Like we said, it's very important just to notice your eating patterns and not try to change them right now. When you start trying to change things too soon, before you have a chance to really understand what you're doing, it's easy to get caught up in the changing and not the noticing. This has the same effect as dieting. Then you stress out about what to do about it. Don't go there. Just let yourself eat or not eat like you usually do.

EMOTIONS AND EATING

I always eat when I'm upset.

— Julie

Eating when you're upset is common. It happens to a lot of people. Maybe someone gave you cookies when you fell down and got hurt. Or if we were sad, we thought that we would feel better if we ate. When we got sick, someone gave us food to make us "stronger" whether we were hungry or not. When we felt like life was out of control, we felt stronger and more powerful when we stopped eating at all.

Remember that there is usually a good reason you do the things you do. You have learned to take care of yourself by either eating or not eating. Both are responses to stresses in your life.

Julie discovered that food calmed her down when she was upset. It was understandable for her to turn to food at those times. Later, she learned to take care of herself in other ways. She learned to listen to herself when she was upset and deal with her feelings in more helpful ways. This took time and patience on her part, but now when she's upset, she can work it out without food.

When I get mad at my parents, I don't want to eat. It takes me a long time to stop being mad. So sometimes I go all day long or longer without eating. This makes them angry at me but I don't care. They shouldn't make me so mad.

— Bret

Bret's way of coping with her anger is to ignore her own hunger for long periods of time. And a part of her liked that she could make her parents mad by not doing what they wanted her to do. The problem with this was she often went hungry. And many times the problems between her and her parents just got worse. As she learned how to deal effectively with her anger in the moment, she didn't have to starve, nor did she have to punish her parents by her behavior.

We naturally change the behaviors that don't work for us when we understand what we're doing in the first place. For now, just try to feel your feelings as much as possible while you notice what you are doing about them.

TRY THIS: Noticing Your Feelings

Today try to be conscious of what emotions you are feeling. When you are hungry, notice what you are feeling physically and emotionally. When you are full, notice what you are feeling physically and emotionally. Whenever you are doing any of the behaviors related to your eating disorder, try just to notice what emotions you are feeling. You may not be able to identify exactly what the feeling is, and that's okay. Don't try to change what you are doing or feeling. Just be aware.

BODY SENSATIONS AND EATING

Since I was a little girl, I've had stomachaches. I think it was because of my dad leaving when I was two. My mom said I would cry myself to sleep and say my tummy hurt. I had to just get over it, though, because it didn't change anything. My mom just felt guilty and my dad didn't come back. So when I started trying to feel my stomach hunger, at first all I felt was the old familiar pain of my childhood stomachaches.

— Cindy

This is a great example of the difference between physical hunger and emotional hunger. Cindy learned how to stop listening to her stomach because it hurt too much and she couldn't do anything about the pain. Now she is learning to separate the two hungers and work appropriately with each of them.

Cindy started letting herself feel her body from the *inside*. She focused her attention on how she felt in her head, her throat, her chest, and her stomach. She asked herself several times a day, whenever she felt hungry, these questions: Am I hungry? Am I physically hungry? Am I emotionally hungry?

For a long time she wasn't sure what she was feeling. But she kept asking the questions and pretty soon the answers came.

TRY THIS: Noticing Body Sensations

Today let yourself feel your body from the inside. Be conscious of what your stomach feels like when it tells you that it's hungry. Let it tell you when it's satisfied and when it's full. Just notice if you feel pain or discomfort when you haven't eaten for awhile. What does it feel like when you eat something you really, really like? Remember, this is just paying attention to body sensations and all of these sensations are fine. Each one has something to teach you. Be open to the teaching.

BECOMING AWARE OF DIET TALK

When me and my girlfriends get together, we just always say how fat we are and how fat everyone else is and how much we ate and how much everyone else eats and how many fat grams are in everything and how much we wished we weighed and how much weight we want to lose and how much better things will be when that happens. It really gets to me sometimes.

— Shauna

If you were born into this culture, you have learned a coded way of talking. We call this *diet talk*. Girls use this coded way of talking more than boys only because they have been around it more. The women in their lives have talked about food and dieting so much that they believe this is the only way to relate to each other. What makes it worse is that after a while it becomes internal and the only way they relate to themselves. Every meal they eat and every pound they weigh is judged as wrong.

Shauna's whole peer group was obsessed with food, fat, and weight. More crucial things like school, work, or play were forgotten or considered less important than the diet talk. As she became aware it, diet talk started to bother her. She realized that it was a waste of time and energy. Since she *learned* this way of speaking with others and with herself, she can also *unlearn* it.

TRY THIS: Noticing Body Sensations

Begin to become aware how many times you worry about your weight, or what you ate, or what you might eat.

Notice how many times you weigh yourself and what you say to yourself when you see the number on the scale. How often do you and your friends talk about dieting in order to lose weight?

How often do you call yourself fat? Or gross? How do you feel about yourself when you do that? How often do you judge others because of their weight? How does that feel?

As we hope you've learned from this chapter, it is important not to criticize or judge these thoughts. The important thing is to notice them. Later, you will learn ways to do things differently. Right now, as gently and as nicely as you can, just observe and accept where you are.

DO IT FOR YOURSELF!

I came to the teen group because my mom and my therapist made me. I had just been diagnosed with anorexia and I had to go see a therapist and go to a support group. I didn't want to at all. But I went because I didn't have a choice. I sat there listening to the other girls, thinking that none of them were like me, nobody understood, and that I was not going to talk. I told my mom after every group that it was horrible, worthless, and that I hated it. I was mad that she made me go and I didn't want her to think that it was in any way a good idea. Then one day I listened to someone in the group talk about how she was so busy rebelling against what her parents wanted her to do, that she didn't even know what she wanted to do. I realized then that I was not alone.

— Celeste

Sometimes when family or friends are worried about your health, they ask you to do certain things. This is because they care and are concerned about you. Whatever they try to make you do, they usually are doing it because they think it is best for you and will help you. This can set up either a *power struggle* in which you want to rebel against what they ask you to do, or a *pleasing struggle* in which you want to do it for them. Neither of these are as important as finding what *you* want to do for *yourself.*

Recovering from struggles with food and weight is not easy. It means giving up behaviors that you have relied on to take care of yourself. It means discovering thoughts and feelings that may be uncomfortable. It means getting to know yourself as who you are, not who you think you should be. And it means getting your self and your life back. In order to do this, you must be willing to fight for yourself.

When you can find the part of yourself that you love and that is worth fighting for, you will also find the voice that knows you want to live and be healthy and happy. Then you will be able to take responsibility for doing this recovery *for yourself.*

All I could hear for the longest time was this voice in my head saying I would be okay if I was thin. Whenever I felt bad, this voice told me I was too fat. To make myself feel better, I would go on a diet and try to lose weight. The obsession with what I ate and being thin took over — there was no room left for me. I didn't even know who I was anymore. Someone asked me, "What do you, Melissa, really believe?" and I didn't know. I had to search really hard to find out what I, Melissa, felt and thought. But I found that I did have feelings and thoughts that were different from all of the obsession with being thin. They were just so hidden.

— Melissa

At first this voice may be very small and hard to hear. It may be buried beneath the voices of self-hatred, self-doubt, or self-praise for being thin and dieting. The first step is finding it, and the second step is nurturing it — helping it to grow and become stronger. This exercise will help you get in touch with the part of you that wants to fight for your life and your happiness.

TRY THIS: Finding Your Will

You will need some pens and paper to write and/or draw. You may want to do this with a parent, friend, or therapist. Or if you do it alone, you may want to talk about it afterward with someone.

1. Close your eyes and get in touch with the part of you that struggles with food and weight. Listen to the messages it gives you. What does it tell you about what you should or shouldn't eat? What does it say about how you should look? What does it want you to do or not do? Imagine what this part of you looks like. When you're done, write down the messages that you heard and, if you want, draw what this part of you looks like.

2. Close your eyes again and get in touch with the part of you that loves you, that cares about you, that likes to be in the world and have fun, that wants to live. Listen

to the messages that it gives you. What does it tell you about who you are as a special person? What does it say about what you really love to do for fun? What does it say about wanting to live? Imagine what this part of you looks like. When you're done, write down the messages that you heard and, if you want, draw what this part of you looks like. Sometimes, because this part is so buried, it is hard to hear the answers. That's okay. Just try, and see what happens.

3. Look at the differences between these two parts. They are both parts of you that need to be heard and understood. Usually, however, the second part gets buried beneath the obsession with the eating disorder.

It's not easy to begin recovering from an eating disorder. As we've said before, it can be scary, overwhelming, and hard work. We know, however, that it is possible because we ourselves have recovered and have witnessed lots of teens and adults recover and get their lives back. The first steps are usually the hardest. Becoming aware of what you are doing, thinking, and feeling may sometimes be difficult, but it is important because it helps you understand who you are and what you need. Once you know this, life becomes much more fun and fulfilling.

It's the Only Body You Have

Your Body — What It Needs

I thought I was doing just fine. I was running track, keeping up with everyone on the team, getting thin, eating low-fat foods, and trying to be really healthy. Even though people commented on how thin I was getting and my parents kept bugging me about eating more, I was sure they didn't know what they were talking about. Then one day I fainted while running, and the next thing I know I was in the hospital. I was there for ten days while they tried to stabilize me. They were treating me for anorexia. I was very, very sick. As I look back now I can see how my desperate emotional need to be thin, and to control my food and my body by dieting, completely overruled my physical need for food. I was so out of touch with listening to what my body needed because I was convinced that the most important thing was to be thin.

— Gina

Your body is an important part of who you are, and listening to what your body needs to grow and be healthy is a necessary part of life. Your body grows faster in your teen years than at any other time in your life, except infancy. You are also going through cognitive, emotional, and hormonal changes. This means that your body has a greater need for specific nutrients. Your body needs lots of calories, vitamins, and minerals to maintain healthy development and to function at its best. Unfortunately, many young girls start dieting just when their body needs food the most! Studies show that 90 percent of high school junior and senior girls diet regularly, and 80 percent of eleven-year-old girls diet. Why do you think that at a time when girls' bodies need lots of food and calories to stay healthy, they go on a diet?

We believe it is caused by the cultural obsession with thinness and dieting. This obsession puts so much pressure on teens and preteens that they feel the best way to be liked and accepted is to be thin, and the best way to get thin is to diet. The need to diet and be thin has become common among young girls as they shift from girlhood into womanhood. This is frightening because *dieting is dangerous* and *dieting rarely works!* Studies show that 95 percent of all dieters regain the weight they lost within one to five years. Although dieting may help you lose weight temporarily, you will most likely gain the weight right back.

What do we actually mean by dieting? EDAP (Eating Disorders Awareness and Prevention) defines dieting and the diet mentality like this:

- *Dieting:* Any attempts in the name of weight loss, "healthy eating," or body sculpting to deny your body the essential, well-balanced nutrients and calories it needs to function to its fullest capacity.
- *Dieting mindset:* When dissatisfaction with your natural body shape or size leads to a decision to actively change your physical body weight or shape.

Dieting is also harmful to your body, mind, and sense of well-being. Let's look at some of the reasons dieting is dangerous:

- *Dieting keeps you from getting the necessary nutrients for healthy development.*
- *Dieting can have serious negative health effects.* Cycles of gaining and losing weight can lead to increased risk of heart disease and long-lasting negative impacts on other body systems. Dieters may also experience

  ❖ loss of muscular strength and endurance
  ❖ weak bones
  ❖ decreased oxygen utilization
  ❖ thinning hair
  ❖ loss of coordination
  ❖ dehydration and electrolyte imbalances
  ❖ fainting, weakness, and slowed heart rates
  ❖ absence of the menstrual cycle

- *Dieting can mess up your metabolism.* When you diet, your body thinks you are starving, so it wisely begins to conserve energy and store fat to help you survive. This slows down your metabolism, which makes it difficult to lose weight.
- *Dieting affects your mind, slowing down reaction times and making it more difficult to concentrate.*
- *Dieting leads to stress, anxiety, and obsessions about food and weight, which limits the brain's working memory capacity.*
- *Dieting is linked with depression and low self-esteem.*
- *Dieting can lead to increased food intake, binge eating, and eating disorders.*
- *Diets don't make you fit.*
- *Diets can make you afraid of food.*

So, basically, diets stink. They're not good for your body, mind, or soul. This may be hard to hear if you have built your whole life around the need to diet. You might begin to feel a slight panic rising, as you think, "But if I can't diet, what can I do?"

Giving up dieting can be difficult and scary. We know that because, after years of using dieting and the obsession with dieting to control our bodies and our world, it felt impossible to stop. Don't worry — there is another way to take care of your food and body that isn't dieting. It is possible to gently and slowly shift away from the destructive cycle of dieting and learn to listen to the needs of your own unique body. This way of intuitive eating will give you back your authority to choose what is best for you and your body.

YOUR BODY ISN'T STUPID

I remember one time my mom made a bunch of brownies for a party we were having and I got into trouble because I ate almost all of them. But all day, all I had was some yogurt, and when I saw those brownies, I couldn't help myself. I guess I was really hungry!

— Josie

Josie's body wasn't stupid, Josie's body was hungry. When we go so long with little or no food, our body just needs to eat — anything it can. At that point it really doesn't matter if it gets brownies, pasta, chips, or salad. It also doesn't matter if the food is intended for a party, food that has been labeled "bad" or "good," or "fattening" food. The body just knows that it is out of fuel and it needs more fuel to keep running. This hunger response can be very stressful to our bodies. It takes us to a place beyond choice and the ability to listen to what our bodies really need.

Our bodies are like machines, precise, intricate, great machines. And, like all machines, they require some kind of outside power in order to work. Computers need electricity, cars need gas, windmills need wind, and bodies need food.

As babies, we learn that when we're hungry and if we cry, someone will give us something to eat. Then when we get enough to eat, we turn our face away and stop. If we don't like what we're given to eat, we spit it out. This is how babies eat. Babies are natural eaters.

However, sometimes the adults in our lives are dealing with their own issues with food, fat, and weight, and we learn to distrust our bodies and our appetites. If the people around us have forgotten how to be natural eaters, it is hard to remember on our own. The way out of an eating disorder is to let ourselves eat and remember how to be natural eaters. This sounds easier than it is.

Remembering how to be a natural eater takes patience and trust. It also takes forgetting what you've been told about food, fat, and weight, and letting yourself discover who you are as a natural eater. Giving yourself permission to find out what you like to eat, how full or empty your body likes to be, and which food is your personal favorite is what this process is all about.

EATING WHEN YOU ARE HUNGRY, EATING WHAT YOUR BODY WANTS, AND STOPPING WHEN YOU ARE FULL

I would go to school without breakfast and not eat anything all day and then eat a little tiny bit at dinner and FEEL PROUD OF MYSELF!!! Like, "All right, I hardly ate anything today!" Now I think about how hungry I was and how miserable that made me and I can't believe it. Trusting myself enough to eat at all was a huge thing. And then trusting myself enough to stop dieting was the next hardest thing, but the most scary was to learn to eat every time I was hungry, eat exactly what I wanted, and stop right when I was full. That was big.

— April

Eating when you are hungry, eating what your body wants, and stopping when you are full are big challenges. To trust yourself enough to do each of these things is a step-by-step process. How in the world do you begin? First, stop dieting. Stop dieting right now. You may not know this but you have a right to eat. You have a right to have hungers, desires, and needs. In this culture you have been taught to disconnect from your own hunger and from your own body. The diet industry, which sells diet foods, plans, and supplements to people like us, makes about 33 billion dollars a year. It is highly invested in not letting you know that you can trust your own body when it comes to food, eating, and weight. We are a society obsessed with thinness and dieting. Everyone talks and thinks about it all the time. The media, your parents, and your teachers have all been taught by society that diets work. They pass on to you the myth that diets work even if diets don't work and never will.

The other way we have gotten disconnected from our hungers is by covering up our feelings. We have used food, either overeating it or undereating it, in order to cope with situations in our lives that we don't know how to cope with. We learned that when we binge or starve we seem to feel better. The truth is we don't feel better for long. Sooner or later eating or not eating this way stops working. We are left with the feelings we were trying not to feel. In addition, we now have eating behaviors that hurt us. When this happens, remember to go back to square one and ask yourself, "Am I hungry? What am I hungry for? Am I full? What do I need? How can I take care of myself?" This takes patience, compassion, and understanding. So, stop dieting, stop starving, stop counting calories, stop obsessing about fat grams, and start living.

EATING WHEN YOU ARE HUNGRY

I never get hungry but I'm always eating. Food is such a BIG DEAL in my house because everyone is always on a diet. So if there's food around and I am around, then I just eat it as fast as I can. If I don't, someone else will or it will be thrown away. I'm afraid to feel my hunger because it might not be at the right time for everyone else.

— Mia

Mia will have to set some boundaries in her household about food. This is hard, especially if her parents are always dieting. But she can still do this part of the program, even if they don't change at all. The important thing for now is to get a clear signal of hunger and then to feed herself as soon as she feels that signal.

The first step of this process begins with the body. We need to *listen* and to *feel* how our bodies tell us that they are physically hungry. We call this stomach hunger. It is different from emotional hunger and spiritual hunger, which we call mouth hunger.

Stomach hunger is a physical sensation that is different for everyone. You may feel it in your stomach, your throat, or you may feel light-headed. The sensation may be subtle or it may be really strong. It may be a pain or just a "funny" feeling somewhere in your body. It is as unique as you are and will help you to distinguish between what your *body* wants and what your *head* wants.

Mouth hunger is more of an emotional feeling, but there can be a physical *feeling* need to put something in your mouth. It is a sensation that you "just have to have something" and it doesn't even matter what it is. When that hunger is active, it's usually reaching for a food that is known as a "binge" food. This isn't wrong, the food that you are wanting is not illegal, and you are not bad because of this. You've just learned how to take care of yourself this way. In time you will know other ways of taking care of yourself, but now is the time to work on being able to tell the difference between eating from physical (stomach) hunger and eating from emotional or spiritual (mouth) hunger.

Everyone is different and every body is different. It's crazy that we should all eat at 8 A.M, 12 noon, and 6 P.M. We are all different sizes and different body types. We have different likes and dislikes. Your parents are different from you and from each other. If you think it would help, give your parents this book, and let them know what you are trying to do.

TRY THIS: Eating When You Are Hungry

1. Pick a day that you don't have to go to school or work or practice and let yourself feel your own hunger. See if you can wait until you get a strong signal. Everyone has a "hunger signal." Yours might be small, or faint, or you might not know what it is at all. Some people's hunger signals are deep in their stomachs, others' are in their throats; Still others just get a little lightheaded when their bodies are trying to tell them they are hungry. The point is to get in touch with your very own hunger signal and know what it is.

2. When you get a clear signal, stay with it for a moment. Let yourself experience how your body tells you it is hungry and what your body feels like when it's hungry. Is it comfortable or uncomfortable to feel hunger in your body? Understanding your hunger is valuable information that you will use your whole life long.

EATING WHAT FEELS GOOD IN YOUR BODY

Everyone told me that if I ate only what I wanted, I would only eat "junk food." And I thought that about myself, too. But when I really listened to my body, I found out that I wanted a lot of other kinds of food. I couldn't believe it the first time I wanted a salad. I really wanted a salad. Not because I was supposed to, not because I should, not because that's what's "good" but because that's what I wanted. Even though I could have any kind of food; candy, burgers, chips, whatever. At that moment my body wanted a salad and I heard it!

— Shannon

For Shannon, the thrill of figuring out what she wanted to eat was validating, exciting, and new. Why is this? We think it's because, in this culture, we are not always taught that we know what is best for us to eat. We live in a diet-obsessed culture. There is a lot of information out there about what to eat, when to eat, and how much to eat. Whole groups of foods are labeled "good" or "bad." Teens and adults we work with have all kinds of beliefs and rules about foods, and we've discovered these aren't necessarily true. When the only information we get comes from companies who make their money selling us their products, we are not getting the whole picture. They are telling us to listen to them and not to our bodies.

Information on nutrition is valuable, but we also have to realize that each person is different. This means that each person's nutritional needs are different, too. There are many nutritionists now who understand how important intuitive eating is. They can help you figure out which dieting rules aren't helpful, and how to eat intuitively and still meet your own body's nutritional needs. The challenge is to figure out what your individual body needs and wants to eat. Listening to your body and understanding what food it needs is much more rewarding than listening to what the diet industry thinks you need. Your body has a definite wisdom that will let you know how many calories, fat grams, carbohydrates, and liquids you need. Trust and have faith in your body. It won't let you down. Diets are information that comes from outside of us. Knowing exactly what foods your body wants is information from inside of yourself.

TRY THIS: Eating What Feels Good in Your Body

1. Say to yourself, "Body, now that you are hungry, what would you like to eat?" Ask yourself if you want something sweet. Salty? Gooey? Crusty? Do you want some protein? Or some veggies? Bread or pasta? Or do you want a combination of all of these? Whatever it is, try to get this food for yourself. It might not be possible to have exactly what you want, but try to get as close as possible. Let go of the many contradictory messages you may have gotten from the society that you live in and stay connected to your body, your hunger, and your satisfaction.

2. Now experience how this food feels in your body. Is it satisfying? Is it what you wanted or not? How does your body feel after you've eaten it?

3. Write down all of your rules and beliefs about different foods. How do these rules and beliefs affect what you eat? Where did you learn them? Try to find someone who is knowledgeable about nutrition and find out if these are helpful or harmful rules and beliefs.

STOPPING WHEN YOUR BODY IS FULL

Stopping when full was really, really hard for me. I was so used to just eating everything on my plate even if I didn't want to. My parents have a real thing about this, so I thought I had to "clean my plate." But when I explained what I was doing, then it was okay. Then I found out that I would just keep eating anyway. So then I went back to asking myself, "Am I hungry still?" or "Can I stop eating yet?" That helped me get back into the moment and I could figure out what was really going on with me. I also realized that sometimes after I ate, I didn't know what else to do with my time. If I was eating, I wasn't bored. I ate a lot of the time when I was bored. This was good to find out.

— Peggy

Peggy learned a lot about her patterns around food when she tried to do this part of the process. She saw where she learned to keep eating, even after she was full (her family) and she also saw why sometimes she would keep eating, even after she was full (boredom). The more she stopped herself in the moment and asked herself where she was and what she was thinking, the more information she got about stomach hunger and mouth hunger. When we're eating out of mouth hunger it's impossible to get a signal from our body about when to stop. That only comes from satisfying physical hunger with food. If we're eating for reasons other than physical hunger, we have to talk ourselves through an emotional process. That's when the question "What do I really need?" becomes so valuable. When we realize we are eating out of mouth hunger, we can ask ourselves what it is that we really need. It comforts us to know we care enough about ourselves to ask, that we are listening, and trying to help ourselves with the troubles or boredom of our lives.

It is not unusual for people to have a hard time with this part. We have to believe that it is our bodies that know when enough is enough. We also have to figure out what else we can do besides eat when we're bored, sad, upset, or happy. We will talk about this in another chapter, but for now remember that stopping when your body is full is often the most difficult part. You can do it. Give yourself time. Be patient and compassionate and you will get there.

TRY THIS: Stopping When Your Body Is Full

1. Just like the hunger signal that you've gotten in touch with, get in touch with your fullness signal. Trust that it is there, even if you don't realize it yet. It usually has a strong stomach feeling but sometimes it's in your mouth or elsewhere in your body. Like the other signals of hunger and what you want to eat, the feeling of fullness is unique and truly belongs to you and you alone.

2. When you feel that signal, ask yourself, "Body, is it all right to stop eating now? Do you want more of this food? Do you want something else?" If you find you are stopping before you feel full, ask yourself, "Why am I not allowing myself to eat until I'm satisfied?"

3. Let yourself stop eating as soon as you are full, knowing that as soon as you're hungry again you can eat. It is now and will always be perfectly fine to eat. However, if you feel that you need to keep eating, even though you are no longer physically hungry, acknowledge *that* to yourself. Don't beat yourself up or yell at yourself. Just keep checking in, asking yourself, "Can I stop eating yet?"

It's the Best Body for You

I was always obsessing about the models in the magazines. I couldn't believe how skinny they were and how fat I was compared to them. Even though I didn't stop eating or start throwing up, I still obsessed about everything I ate and how I looked all the time.

— Kate

Obsessing about the "perfect" body is a horrible way to live. It takes up time and energy you could be spending on going to the beach, hanging with your friends, listening to music, doing your schoolwork, or playing your sport. When the obsession to look perfect is in charge of your life, there is no room for your life.

Just as you were born with a natural appetite that tells you when you're hungry, what you want, and when you're full, you were also born with a natural body that is the perfect size for you. Genetics determine your body shape and size. We are programmed by our genetic code to be a certain height, weight, and build. If we try to fight it, we can get really sick. We can develop low self-esteem, be very unhappy with our bodies, or get an eating disorder.

Our opinions about what is beautiful are swayed by what the media dictates. Consider this: Less than 2 percent of the women in this country naturally look like the models you see in *Sassy, Vogue, Cosmopolitan,* or *Seventeen.* Less than 2 percent! That means that the chances of having a model's height, weight, and looks without starving yourself or having cosmetic surgery are practically nonexistent.

When you grow up in a culture like ours, one that is obsessed with dieting and thinness, it is natural to assume that everyone everywhere is just as obsessed with dieting and being thin. You don't know any other way of being until somehow you get a different perspective, maybe by looking at history, at other cultures, or even by dreaming about other possibilities. Other ways of thinking do exist, much healthier, loving ways of thinking that do not continually tear us down and make us question our personal value. All we know, however, is what we learn from our culture, which keeps us feeling bad about ourselves most of the time.

Usually these messages come in the form of an advertisement in which you are being sold a product. It could be clothes, perfume, cigarettes, alcohol, food, diets, exercise equipment, magazines, cars, makeup, restaurants, or just about anything. Advertisers try to convince you that you *need* this product. They suggest that you are not okay the way you are but if you just buy their product you'll have a perfect life. Think about the ads you've seen: the woman who has lost weight on some diet or exercise machine and now her life is perfect; the woman who smokes a cigarette and has her favorite fantasy come true; the woman who wears a certain perfume and all of the men swoon over her; and the man who performs some great athletic feat while wearing a new type of shoe. In every case, a product is supposed to have made someone happy, or better, or more complete.

You may not even be aware these messages are putting pressure on you. After all, you might have been hearing them since you were a baby! Ever since you learned to understand what people were saying, you've been taking in these messages. Some of these messages may have seemed very positive for you, and some may have just made you feel bad about yourself. It is important to begin questioning these messages and how they affect your self-esteem.

If you live your life trying to make yourself look like what the advertisers say you should look like in order to be "beautiful," you will either make yourself very sick in the process or you will always be unhappy because you can never reach an impossible goal. However, if you question the standards that define "beautiful" as tall and thin, and know that you don't have to think the way they think, you can start defining what is right and beautiful for your own unique body.

Let's slow down and take a close look at the messages you receive so that you can start deciding which ones you want to take in and which ones you don't.

TRY THIS: Questioning Cultural Messages

1. Begin by asking yourself where you have learned your beliefs about food and weight. Where did you learn to count calories or fat grams? Where did you learn about what body type is beautiful? Where have you learned to dislike the fat on your stomach, thighs, breasts, buttocks, arms, face, or wherever? Where have you learned to worry about your weight? Where have you learned what weight you supposedly "should" be? What underlying messages do you see in ads and how do they make you feel or act?

2. As you pay attention to these details, you will be able to hear one of these messages instead of just taking it in. Question whether you want to buy into it or call it garbage and throw it out. If you think it's not true or helpful, come up with an alternative message that you believe is true and helpful. Imagine this message on a billboard, in a magazine, on TV. Write it down on a piece of paper or in a journal, and pull it out whenever you need to be reminded.

3. Find a friend who can do this with you. When you are driving around looking at billboards or watching a movie, talk together about what messages you are hearing and what you think of them. Talk about what messages you'd rather be hearing.

ACCEPTING YOUR BODY

I was put on a diet when I was twelve years old. My mom and my sisters are all really tall and thin. I'm shorter and kinda fat. I was teased at school and always thought I was a freak. My parents didn't know what else to do but try to help me by regulating my food. I would hardly eat anything and still I just stayed the same. I even started getting headaches because I would only eat a little all day. My coach said if I didn't eat right, I couldn't play sports anymore. I was scared that I would get even bigger than I already was if I ate. The more my parents tried to control my food, the worse I felt about being so different from everybody else, so the more I ate. I was fourteen, fat, and depressed and the only thing that made me feel better was eating. Then I started listening to my body and finding out when I was hungry, what I wanted to eat, and when I was full. This helped a lot. I realized if I fed myself better, then I got really strong. And I realized that because of my size I can do things that my sisters can't do. That was really great.

— Lisa

If someone told you to "accept your body exactly as it is right now," what would you do? Would you be relieved or would you run in fear? This is exactly what we are saying. We are asking you to give up the pull to have your body conform to the current standard of beauty.

We are also asking you to realize that your body is young and still changing. You may grow taller as you get older. You may stay the same height but you may get bigger breasts and hips. We don't know, nor do you, exactly what you will look like when you are fully grown. Trying to be thinner than you were meant to be is like trying to change your eye color. You may be able to get colored contact lenses, but you would never be able to permanently change it. Our bodies are like that — we may be able to change it for a little while, but not forever.

Learning to accept your body as it is now is very hard. It may feel like you're giving up. And in a way you are. You're giving up self-hatred, deprivation, and the obsession with food and weight. This is a good thing. It will enable you to live a happier life. Your body is not your enemy. Your food is not your enemy. Many people have been judged by this society as wrong for having a certain body type. But those people are not wrong. The culture's judgment of them is wrong. Our bodies have an intelligence that will steer us in the right direction if we choose to listen. We have to choose our bodies instead of our culture.

If you have been overeating and weigh more than your body naturally wants to weigh, you need to acknowledge and learn to accept that, for now, this is exactly how your body needs to look. It may not look this way forever. When you eat like a natural eater, your body can be free to be its natural size, whatever that size may be, whether it's the cultural ideal or not. Loving and accepting yourself and your body, exactly as it is, is the key to getting through the doors of life.

TRY THIS: Accepting Your Body

A. DRAWING EXERCISE

1. Draw an outline of your body on a piece of paper. Color the parts of your body that you don't like. Use one color for what you don't like and another color for what you do. Don't worry if it's not a "perfect" drawing. The main point is just to see what parts you don't like and what parts you do.

2. Go though each part and see if you can figure out where you got the idea that it is "good" or "bad." What is the message you got? Write down the message next to the body part.

3. With your eyes closed, focus your attention on each of these body parts and ask what the different parts really do for you. For instance: Does your stomach process food for you? Do your legs get you up hills? Does your butt give you something comfortable to sit on?

4. Say thank you to these different body parts. They do a good job even if they don't look like you want them to. Tell them that you are working on accepting them and to hang in there with you while you are doing it.

B. FAMILY HISTORY EXERCISE

Go through pictures and see if you can figure out where your personal body type came from genetically. If you don't have pictures, just know you have an ancestor from a tribe that looked like you. Say thank you to the ancestors that came before you. Realize that your body is the perfect size for you right now. Even if you are not your "natural size," if you keep letting yourself recover you will be.

TRUSTING YOUR BODY

Our bodies are wise. They tell us when we are hungry, what we want to eat, and when we're full. They also tell us when we're tired and need to sleep, and when we want to dance. Our bodies will let us know when we have to go to the bathroom and when we're thirsty. Our bellies will tell us when we're in danger and when we are living our truth. Our bodies are incredible fountains of wisdom. We can learn to trust them to tell us everything. We may not have been taught to listen, but we can learn. The way to learn what our bodies are saying is to learn how to listen.

TRY THIS: Trusting Your Body

It's best to do this exercise on a day when nothing else will be going on. Make a promise to yourself that on this day you will listen to your body and trust it to tell you if you're cold or hot, hungry or not, tired or full of energy, and at ease within yourself or uncomfortable. If you are cold, turn up the heat. If you are hot, let yourself get cool. If you are hungry, eat. And if you're full, stop eating. Give yourself permission to sleep when you are tired and take yourself out for exercise if you have the energy. If you have something making you uncomfortable, see if you can ease the pain. Dedicate this whole day to listening to and answering your own body.

At the end of this day, write down in your journal what this day felt like to you. What was different about this day from other days? What was the same? Write about the differences you would like to make more permanent. For instance, did you realize that you need more sleep than you usually allow yourself to have? Did your body want to move more or less than usual? Did you want more or less food than usual? Was it harder or easier to trust your body than you thought?

Just let yourself write. Write about what you felt and what you discovered about yourself today. If you can, promise yourself that you will begin to make the changes your body is asking you to make.

Trust yourself, trust your body. As long as you are alive and on this planet, your body is your home.

STOP BEATING YOURSELF UP

When I started to notice how I talked to myself in my head, I couldn't believe how mean I was to myself. I was always telling myself that my legs were too fat, my face was too puffy, and I was too ugly to be liked by anyone. I was so insecure that I started saying these things out loud to my friends just so I could hear them say back to me that they weren't true. It was a big relief when I learned to stop beating myself up and start treating myself like a friend.

— Sophia

Would you talk to your best friend the way you talk to your body and to yourself? We doubt it. Usually we are much harder on ourselves than others. As you become aware of the negative way you talk to yourself, it is important to begin to change it. Talking to yourself in a mean way is not only unproductive, it is hurtful and damaging. It can make you feel worse, rather than better, and can lead to destructive behavior. If you can stop your negative self talk and learn to talk to yourself in a more supportive, nurturing way, you will feel better about yourself and have more room to find solutions to your problems.

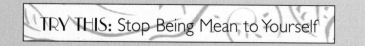

TRY THIS: Stop Being Mean to Yourself

1. Pick a day when you don't have a lot going on and try be become aware of when you say negative things to your body or yourself (for example, "I can't believe how fat my legs are," or "That was such a stupid thing you said!").
2. As soon as you hear yourself say something mean, try stopping it. Say to yourself something like "Oops, I'm beating myself up again and that's not okay anymore."

3. Try to come up with something else to say that is less negative, or even positive. If that's too hard, try to think of what you might say to a friend. For example, "These are my legs and they are just the way they are," or "Well, I did the best I could."

It will probably feel very uncomfortable at first to say something nice to yourself. It may feel like you are being silly or stuck-up. That is only because you have become so accustomed to being critical of yourself that it feels different. However, as you practice this exercise, it will become easier to be nice to yourself, and it will free up a lot more energy to have fun.

You're More Than Meets the Eye

As we've said before, we have learned in this culture to look at our bodies as if they were objects to be sculpted into a perfect body type that has nothing to do with our own natural and unique bodies. When most females look in their mirrors, their attention is drawn to those parts of their body they hate, and how they can change their clothes, makeup, or body to "fix" what they don't like. We've lost the ability to see within ourselves what lies beyond the expectations of what we "should" look like. The next exercise teaches us to see beyond what we think we "should" be, to who we really are.

TRY THIS: Seeing Your True Self

1. Stand in front of a full-length mirror, with clothes on or off. (If you don't have one, just use the biggest one you have.)

2. Begin by looking into your eyes. Try to get beyond looking at what your eyes look like, and actually see yourself in your eyes. Say hello to yourself.

3. Starting with your face, notice what is uniquely yours. Notice the shape of your eyes and eyebrows, the fullness of your cheeks, the size and shape of your nose and mouth, and how your hair falls over your face, head, and/or shoulders. Try to look at your face as if you were an artist — not judging it as right or wrong, but exploring the colors, shapes, sizes, and qualities. *Whenever a negative or critical thought comes up, look back into your eyes, take a deep breath, let go of the thought, and try again.*

4. Using the same technique, look at your arms, breasts, belly, legs, and the rest of your body. Once again, just look generally at the size, shape, texture, and qualities of your body parts. If a negative thought comes up, look back into your eyes, take a deep breath, let go of the thought, and try again.

When you start to feel tired or overwhelmed, stop. This shouldn't feel like torture. The first time you do this you may only be able to do it for three minutes, looking only at your face. But if you do it every day, it will become easier and easier to look at your body with nonjudgmental eyes. And don't forget — as you rise in the morning and look at yourself for the first time in the mirror, look in your eyes and say hello to yourself!

HANGING OUT IN YOUR BODY

If you struggle with food and weight, most likely you spend a lot of time in your head, worrying about what you should or shouldn't eat, and what you should or shouldn't look like. Being in our heads and thinking over and over about things is called obsessing. Obsessing about food and weight keeps us from being in our bodies and from feeling the different physical sensations that are key to understanding who we are and what we need. It's important to learn to relax our minds and be present with what's happening in our bodies. Here is an exercise to help you let go of the obsessive thoughts and be present in your body.

TRY THIS: Body Time

1. Find a quiet place where you can sit down and relax with no one to disturb you.
2. Get as comfortable as you can, lying down or sitting in a comfortable chair. Close your eyes if you wish and start by paying attention to your breathing. Notice what it feels like to breathe in through your nose, chest, and belly and out again. Don't try to change your breathing, just notice the natural rhythm of your breathing.
3. Every time your mind wanders off to think about something, just bring your awareness back to your breath. Don't worry if you have to do this a million times! It will get easier as you practice this.
4. Scanning your body from your head to your toes, notice what each body part feels like. Do you have any aches or pains anywhere? Does any part feel relaxed or anxious? Is there any part that is more difficult to feel than others? What sensations do you feel in each part?
5. Check in with your body and notice how it feels overall. Are you tired, energetic, stressed, relaxed, hungry, full, warm, cold?

6. Bring your awareness back to your breath. Take a moment just to rest in your own unique body. Feel what it feels like to be in your body and aware of your body.

When you are ready, you can open your eyes. How do you feel? Throughout every day, remember that when you feel yourself caught up in obsessive thoughts about food and weight, you can take a few deep breaths, bring your awareness into your body, and check in with yourself.

SEXUALITY

I think there's this really crazy idea that you're only allowed to feel sexual if you look a certain way. Like if only you're thin enough, or if only your skin is beautiful enough, then you're allowed to pursue whoever you are interested in. Part of my eating disorder was to feel okay being sexual. It was okay to feel sexual when I was thin, but not when I was fat.

— Vanessa

Understanding your sexuality is a big part of becoming a teenager. How you feel about your body plays a major role in how you express your sexuality. There are many different beliefs in our culture about how you should and shouldn't behave sexually. Trying to figure out what is right for you can be challenging. We, as females, have to question which beliefs about our sexuality are helpful and which are harmful. For example, the current cultural standard, that thin women with big breasts are sexy, is harmful. All women are capable of being sexy no matter what their body type. The more important standard that we as a society should strive for is one that asks the question: "How do we *want to feel* in our bodies — physically, intellectually, emotionally, spiritually, and sexually?" Asking this question and listening to the voice within is a much more powerful way to begin to look at the glorious world of sex.

Many times in the Beyond Hunger groups when the subject of sex comes up, all the voices go silent. Why is it so hard and so confusing to talk about sex? One of the reasons is because of the way that our culture views the body and sexuality. Women are not encouraged to express their sexuality in a healthy, pleasurable way. Our culture objectifies bodies and sex. That means society has separated the sacred, the spiritual, and the emotional qualities from our bodies and sexuality, and uses what is left for financial or other gains. Our culture looks at bodies and sex as objects and acts that can be used, molded, or sold for whatever we want. Sex and sexy bodies are used to sell beer, cars, cigarettes, clothes, and perfume. Think about some of the jeans and perfume ads you have seen on television and in magazines. Separating our bodies from their sacredness and using them for commercial purposes creates a feeling that our bodies are not our own, that they belong to someone else. Someone else will tell us how our bodies should be. We all receive on a daily basis — any time we leave the house, turn on the television, or go to the movies — a lot of confusing or conflicting messages about our bodies and sex. There's a lot of bad information out there, but there is also good information (see Resources).

Ever since I can remember my Grandmother used to tell me, "You need to lose weight 'cause if you don't, guys will never look at you"... that was always the message. My Grandpa used to tell me, "Guys don't want big girls, but they don't want really skinny girls either. They want in-between girls." But I started going out and these guys just straight out wanted to have sex with me. I thought, "Is that okay?" And I knew it wasn't okay, but I was like, "Am I supposed to have sex because they like me for how I look?" So it was really confusing because it was like, "Guys won't like you that way" but they go ahead and do it anyway? It was a bad kind of attention but it was the kind of attention that I thought I was supposed to get. But then I finally found someone I really loved. . . . When I did have sex, I was really happy with it and felt good about it. . . . When you get the good attention, the loving attention, that is the best thing ever.

— Cindy

Over and over we hear the same feelings about the subject of sex and sexuality. The main feelings that come up are shame and guilt: *shame* that the girls are not good or pretty enough to enjoy their bodies in a sexual way, and *guilt* for having sexual feelings in the first place. Another feeling that is often brought up is the feeling of being taken advantage of, or not being made aware of what was going on in a sexual situation. Many girls and women give in to the pressure to do sexual things they aren't ready to do. As a result, they often feel that *they* are bad or wrong. Girls have a right to say no, feel good about what they have said, and have it be respected. Girls also have a right to say yes, and to feel good about that as well.

We get tons of messages telling us how to think about sex, how to behave, what is good or bad. They are mostly someone else's opinions. Added to these messages are the messages that the *natural body*, with all its smells, bumps, imperfections, fat, and blemishes, is bad. We listen to these messages and we think that maybe other people know more than we do about what we need and what we want. We think maybe we should be thinking the way they are thinking. This takes us away from our own truth about how we really feel about our bodies and sex. How in the world could anyone have a pleasurable sexual experience with all these negative opinions floating around? It's not easy, that's for sure.

The first step in figuring this all out is to sort through all the different ideas and messages you have gotten and see if they honestly work for you. You might have learned about sex through a variety of sources — TV, magazines, movies, novels, family, schools, and friends. A lot of the information is probably true and correct. This is good. But if you are like most kids, a lot of what you have learned is a lot of bunk. This is not so good. Many adults have a hard time talking honesty about sex because they are terrified of the subject or have been given bad information themselves.

Most of my issues with food and weight centered around my need for male attention and affirmation and that whole kind of thing, which is really scary for me. My mother is really beautiful and I grew up hearing that she is so great looking and everything. I think that a lot of my intentions were that way, like people commenting about my looks, saying you're so sexy, you're so sexy. And I loved hearing it — I couldn't hear it enough. And I thought if I did hear it enough I would feel that way, but I never did. It took looking at myself and realizing that I would never feel that way until I could love myself.

— Kate

In the society we live in today, we honor the slim, the pretty, the sexy, the young, the blonde, and the white. What happens if you are a person who is not slim, pretty, sexy, young, blonde, and white? Chances are your self-esteem suffers. Chances are you start to believe that your whole self-worth as a lively, important sexual person is less than zero. So you might think that a little plastic surgery here, or a little dieting or makeup there, might make you happy. And when it doesn't make you feel better (because you haven't addressed the real issue) and only makes you feel worse, then you are really stuck. It then becomes a vicious cycle as you turn to more and more "self-improvement" methods that don't work either. What the real issue is, what you really need to see, is that your looks are not the problem. This is a really important idea to understand. Here is the real issue: Your body is not the problem, your sexuality is not the problem, your physical appearance is not the problem, you are not the problem. The way society views your body and your sexuality is the problem.

What if you were taught that sex was a powerful, wonderful, complicated, joyful, vulnerable, spiritual, and life-affirming experience? What if you were taught that all bodies, girls', boys', women's, and men's, were to be honored, respected, and cherished no matter what size, shape, color, or age? What if you were told the honest truth and then given the tools to make your own choices from within yourself, without any pressure from outside? What if you were supported 100 percent around that choice? Would your sexual life be different?

Believe it or not, there are cultures in the world today that are much more loving and compassionate about sexuality than ours. Before entering puberty, girls and boys are taught an appreciation and respect for sex. The confusion that often comes with young sexual feelings is openly talked about and cleared up. Kids are taught that sex is beautiful, sacred, and pleasurable. In tribal communities this is done with cultural rituals that are designed to give them faith and trust that they will take care of themselves as they step into sexual experiences. In countries that have an honest and open educational forum designed to talk about sex without shame or guilt, young adults are given the knowledge they need in order to make informed choices. This allows them to have a sense of being protected and guided in ways that will empower them.

Yet in this culture, we hear story after story of girls who have had sexual experiences they regret. Instead of feeling powerful, loved, and satisfied, they felt disappointed, disillusioned, numbed out, or wounded. Add to this the notion that the female body is bad, wrong, or needs to be improved on. Then it is no mystery why you as a young girl might feel anxious about becoming a sensual, sexual being.

Sex is a vulnerable, intimate experience when we are in our bodies and consciously aware of what we are feeling. As we open our bodies to being sexual, we open our hearts and our souls to the love we feel for ourselves and our partner. When we are in a relationship of respect and commitment, the love we feel will be mirrored back to us. When this doesn't happen, we usually blame our bodies. This is what we have been taught to do. But blaming our bodies is a lie.

In our groups we teach girls and women to not only accept but actually love their bodies, no matter what they look like. This can break down the barriers of shame and negative body image. It takes a lot of courage, trust, and hard work to face those barriers, break through them, and move against the tide of cultural distrust and hate for the feminine body. But it is well worth it. You have a natural right to own all of yourself, physically, intellectually, emotionally, spiritually, and sexually. The next exercise might help you to begin to do that.

TRY THIS: Exploring Your Sexuality

1. As you are exploring your sexuality, be clear with yourself what behaviors you are comfortable with. You may want the support of a trustworthy adult to help you sort out any questions or concerns you might have. If you are

sexually active, be sure to prepare yourself so that you have what you need to protect yourself from pregnancy and sexually transmitted diseases (see Resources).

2. If you have a partner, think beforehand about what you want and what you feel safe doing. Communicate this clearly. It may be uncomfortable at first, but with practice it will become easier. Listening to each other is a very important step in respecting each other's needs and boundaries. If you are being asked to engage in a certain sexual behavior, ask yourself first if this is comfortable to you. Ask yourself if it might hurt you in any way. If so, take care of yourself by saying no. In a healthy relationship, your partner will respect your decision and listen to you.

3. When you are feeling sexual, instead of being aware of the outside of your body, start to become aware of the feelings inside your body. For instance, instead of wondering how you *look to another person* (fat, squishy, bumpy), wonder how you *feel to yourself* (excited, passionate, uncomfortable). Stay in touch with what you are feeling physically and emotionally. This will allow you not only to feel the pleasure more fully, but also take care of yourself if you are uncomfortable in any way.

4. Throughout the sexual experience, notice if you feel safe, loved, and nurtured by the experience. Healthy sexual experiences should leave you feeling good about your body and yourself. If you don't, question why. Discuss this with someone who can help you sort out why this is happening and what you need to do to take care of yourself. Remember — no matter what your body size — you deserve the right to sexual pleasure and respect for your needs.

Emotions Gone Wild

Fat Is Not a Feeling

When I was in school, I was taught math, English, science, and history. I was never taught feelings. In fact, I was taught just the opposite. The culture and family that I was raised in did not know how to handle feelings, mine or their own. So I learned how to "stuff" my feelings. Starting at a very young age, I would do anything to get away from uncomfortable feelings. Some of those things were more acceptable than others. But regardless of what I did about them, the main thing I was trying to do was get away from them. So I never learned how to just "be" with my feelings and feel them without overeating, undereating, or obsessing about my weight. I often felt as if I was out of control and my emotions were running wild. And if I didn't keep them hidden and out of sight, I would go crazy. It took me years to learn to identify and go through my own feelings without trying to escape them.

— Laurelee

Ask a female in this culture today how she is feeling and it would not be unusual to hear her say, "Fat." Believe it or not, "fat" is not a feeling, yet most females know what "feeling fat" means. It's our secret language for saying that we feel bad, wrong, sad, bored, scared, overwhelmed, or just plain messed up. Because we don't always know how to put our feelings into words, or because we don't want to put them into words, we just say, "I feel fat." But "I feel fat" is more than just an expression of feelings, like "I feel sad," or "I feel scared." "I feel fat" is a criticism of one's self. It is a put-down. We proclaim ourselves and our bodies guilty of something. We decided in a matter of seconds that the feeling of sadness, boredom, anger, or fear made our body wrong. We have not asked ourselves why we are feeling sad. We have not learned any lessons from our sadness. We have not given ourselves the opportunity to act on our sadness.

We have feelings in order to call attention to parts of our lives that need attention. If we ignore our feelings, we neglect ourselves and others and our lives begin to fall apart.

Many of us raised in this culture are clueless when it comes to our own feelings. We are often taught that how we look or how we perform is the most important thing. But really, it is *how we feel* and that *we know how we feel* that will help us get through our lives as nothing else can. If we were told all of our feelings were normal, natural, needed, and welcome, we would grow up knowing our feelings and how to work with them, and through them, with very little effort. Unfortunately, many of us are told or shown something just the opposite.

We have received messages that tell us to "be nice," "be sweet," "look on the bright side," "stop worrying," "stop crying." We're told: " I don't like it when you act like that," "Don't make such a fuss," "You're too sensitive," "Wipe that frown off your face," and "Don't get mad at me, young lady!" So while sometimes these messages are said to us by people who love us and are only trying to help, more often than not they take us away from our feelings and what is really going on inside us. Our feelings go into hiding and then we become embarrassed, ashamed, scared, or separate from them.

What if all of our lives people acknowledged our feelings? For instance, what if, instead of the comments above, we were told things like "Wow, you are really angry, huh?" or "I'm noticing that you seem sad; is there anything I can do for you?" or "You look happy today," or "I'm sorry things are confusing for you right now; do you want to talk about it?" What would have been different about our lives and the many thousands of feelings about our lives, if we were taught how to get in touch and stay in touch with our feelings instead of how to act as if they didn't exist? Probably we would be more at peace with ourselves, our bodies, and our food. While we may not be able to turn back the clock and relive our lives in a different environment, we can relearn how to feel our feelings.

THE MANY DEFINITIONS OF FEELINGS

My struggle is always involved with my father because he wasn't there and disappeared out of my life. So when I started having a battle with food and getting bigger, it was always because of comfort eating. It was "Why doesn't he love me? What did I do wrong?" Food would comfort me. My mom was gone a lot too, so when she wasn't there she was in night school trying to get a degree so she could give me a better life. I was always home baby-sitting, eating junk food. It made me feel better, you know? Junk food can make it go away. I never had a lot of friends. There was nothing really to turn to. It was always about where is the love in my life?

— Tiffany

This young girl had no way to cope with the many painful feelings of loss and loneliness, except by eating. And thank goodness, she had that. It would have been a lot worse for her if she hadn't. As she said, "junk food can make it go away." Eating over her feelings gave her the comfort she needed at the time that she needed it. Later on in her recovery, she found other ways to cope with her feelings, and these new ways worked better than junk food, but that took time, patience, understanding, compassion, and practice.

There are thousands of feelings, thousands of ways to feel those feelings, and thousands of ways to express those feelings. There are feelings that tell us when we are happy and there are feelings that tell us when we are sad. There are feelings of anger and frustration. There are comfortable feelings and there are peaceful feelings. There are many different ways that we react to our feelings. Sometimes we feel like we get lost in the feelings, especially if they are "bad" or difficult feelings. Sometimes we react because our feelings are too intense or strong. Intense feelings, when we do not know how to handle them, can be overwhelming. Strangely enough, sometimes even the so-called "good" feelings are too much for us too.

Feelings are like waves in the ocean; we need to learn how to ride through them and know that they will shift and change. When we know that they will end, we can get through them more easily. We can remind ourselves that this too shall pass, that there is a light at the end of the tunnel. By staying with our feelings and riding the wave, we learn how to feel and process them. When the intensity subsides, and we come out on the other side of our feelings, we are in a position to take some kind of action in response to those feelings. This is different than what we are probably used to doing, which is to react while immersed in the feeling.

What would it have been like if we had been taught how to act from a place of understanding our feelings, instead of reacting from a place of fearing our feelings? For one thing, we would be able to choose what we wanted to do about a particular problem that we might be having. We would have experience in using our intuition and knowledge for making decisions. We would be able to know our own truth about how we feel or think about something. These are skills and pieces of information about ourselves that we desperately need to cope with life and to live life fully.

Another way our lives might have been different had we been taught to act instead of react is that we wouldn't have had to turn to food or the obsession with food and weight to get us through our unfelt or unexpressed feelings. We wouldn't ever have been dependent on undereating or overeating to soothe or calm ourselves. As we've said before, food and the obsession with food and weight is a way to cope that helps us to avoid feeling uncomfortable or unbearable feelings. The disorder sits on top of the feelings and all we worry about is the disorder. We obsess about what we eat or how we look rather than wonder who we are or how we feel. This is the way our eating disorder serves us. Unfortunately, sooner or later, it stops working for us and then we are really stuck. We have the feeling. We have the disorder. And we have no skills to help ourselves out of either one.

The way to get out of the rut is to learn how to accept and feel all of our feelings, every time, no matter what. Here is one way to begin to do this:

TRY THIS: Getting to Know Your Feelings

1. Pick a day when there is not a lot going on with you. Let it be okay to have whatever feelings you have. Don't try to change them or make them better. Just notice them and feel them.

2. As clearly as you can, name your feelings. For instance, you might say to yourself, "What I'm feeling right now is anger." Or maybe you say, "This is what boredom feels like," or "I am happy."

3. The next step is to see where these different feelings live in your body. Do you hold a lot of your feelings in your stomach? Or do you store emotions in your neck and shoulders? Do a simple body scan and see if you can match up the feeling with the place in your body where you first feel it.

4. Ask yourself if this is a feeling that truly belongs to you. In other words maybe what you are feeling is your mother's sadness, your father's boredom, your girl-friend's rage, or your boyfriend's confusion. Sometimes we take on other people's feelings as our own. This is not unusual. However, you can learn to let these feel-ings go.

5. See if some situation or someone triggered this feeling in you. What happened? Can you understand why you would have the reaction that you had?

6. When you have a clear awareness of the feeling, the name of the feeling, the place where the feeling is in your body, and the person or situation that caused it, close your eyes and take a deep breath.

7. Imagine that your feeling is a friend and invite it to sit down next to you or across a table from you. Or let your feeling become an ocean wave and imagine sitting on the beach looking at it.

8. Take another deep breath and let yourself fill up with your own feeling. Feel this feeling from the top of your head to the tip of your toe. As you exhale, let your

feeling move through your body and out. When you are ready, open your eyes, and go on with your day.

Don't be concerned if, at first, it is hard to stay with every feeling you have and to go through the whole exercise with each one. The point is to begin to recognize your feelings and let them all be okay. Don't worry if you can't always identify what you are feeling. Time will bring clarity. No matter how you feel, it is okay. These are your feelings, but they are not you. Your feelings are there for a very important reason. You are human and feelings are one of the things that make you human. However, you are much more than your feelings. *You* are not your feelings.

FEELINGS AND FOOD

What I make of my eating disorder was that it was the only tool that I could use to help me cope with life. There were a lot of problems happening with my family and my life. There was so much stuff going on. I was coming of age and my body was reshaping. That was so hard for me. I didn't know where to turn. I guess the problem was that I had never really gotten a healthy idea of how to deal with all that stuff. I didn't know how to deal with all these feelings I had. I thought I wasn't supposed to have them. I looked to "shrinking" because I didn't know what else to do. The only way that I could sedate those feelings and concentrate on something else was through focusing on not eating. It started out as kind of a tool and then it turned into addiction. Today somebody told me this really neat quote, that "any tool is a weapon if you hold it the right way."

— Vanessa

Vanessa learned how to use a tool that eventually turned into a weapon, a weapon that she used against herself. It's not her fault. Like she said, she "had never really gotten a healthy idea of how to deal with all that stuff." What we are asking you to do is, for now, let the weapon go back to being a tool and see what you can learn from it. Let your need to use food and the obsession with food and weight be okay for now. By giving it permission to exist, you are giving yourself an opportunity to learn. Notice when you are using this tool to cope with your feelings and slowly bring your awareness to what else might work.

If you have not been taught how to recognize and work through your feelings, what we are asking you to do may seem impossible. It's not. It is hard. It is different, but not impossible. It will take time and patience. You are learning a new skill and like any new skill, with understanding and lots of practice, you will get the hang of it. Eventually it will come very naturally to you.

We tell the girls in our groups that after a while they will be glad that they had this disorder because it will work to their advantage once they understand it. Your eating disorder will let you know, more than anything else, when something is "up" for you. Your eating disorder will give you immediate feedback. When you start to obsess about food and weight, consider it a "red flag" to yourself that something is amiss. When you want to eat and you know you're not hungry, consider it a signal that you need to check in with yourself. When you think that you are "so fat, I can't even believe it," you know that a part of you is trying to get your attention. Instead of buying into the lies, stop and ask yourself, "What's up?" Always remember that *it's never about the food, it's never about your weight, it's always about something else.* The food, the weight, and the obsession are covering what is really bothering you.

TRY THIS: Exploring Feelings and Food

1. Notice when a thought comes up about eating, *when you know you are not hungry,* and try to have this dialogue with yourself, "What am I feeling right now? What do I really want? I'm not that hungry right now, so am I needing something that I think only food can give me? What is it? Comfort, fullness, numbness, what? I will give myself everything that is in my power to give myself. Is food the only thing that will satisfy me or is there something else?" Another example might be that maybe you're wanting to binge and eat a bunch of cookies. You know that you are full, but you don't care. You just want to eat them. Ask yourself, "What's up with that? What do I want these cookies to do for me?" Then listen for the answer. Take a few moments to write down the feeling and what you want to do about the feeling.

2. If what you usually do is to undereat, notice when a thought comes up about not eating when you know you are hungry. Have a similar dialogue as the one above. Ask yourself, "Why am I not giving my body and myself food? What do I hope to get by depriving myself?" When you have an answer, write it down.

3. Close your eyes and notice what your body feels like. Do you feel tense? Do you feel tired? Do you feel full of energy? Are you anxious? Where in your body are these feelings that are so tied to eating or not eating?

Are you experiencing emotions that you can't identify or that you don't understand? That's okay. Just gently stay in your body and feel what you are feeling.

4. Keeping your eyes closed, see if you are getting any images or pictures in your head. It could be anything at all. Let it come and just take what's there. This is how your subconscious shows itself to you so don't worry if it doesn't make any logical sense. It's like dreaming: The logical mind doesn't always understand the world of the subconscious. But like with dreaming, if you can unlock the meaning of what you see, you will get a world of self-knowledge. So, see what images come up when you tune into the feeling that is causing your eating problem. Does the image help you identify the feeling? If so, open you eyes and write this down.

5. If you can't come up with the feeling, or you're not in touch with your body, or you aren't getting any images that are helping you, let the exercise go and come back to it another time. Realize that this is a process. It takes time, patience, and compassion to go within and feel your feelings, especially about food and weight.

If this exercise is helpful to you, you will know it. If it is not, don't worry about it. The main thing to keep doing is tuning in and asking yourself what's up. Realize that something is bothering you. Realize that the way that you've been dealing with the things that bother you is to undereat, overeat, or obsess about your weight. Somewhere, you've been taught how to do this. What you haven't been taught is how to stay with yourself, feel your feelings, and not eat or obsess about them. If you knew another way you would already be doing it.

In the beginning, when you are learning to identify feelings and how they can cause you to overeat or undereat, you may get stuck on the top layer. For instance, if you've just binged, you might be mad at yourself for bingeing. This is the top layer of feelings. If you can look deeper into yourself, you may find the underlying feeling that was there to make you binge in the first place.

The same thing is true if you notice that you are hungry, but you won't let yourself eat. You may be angry or disappointed in yourself because you've been trying to eat when you're hungry and for some reason you won't let yourself. If you can look underneath the feelings you have about your eating disorder, you might see what is causing you to want to starve.

Later on in this chapter we will talk about how to process the feelings appropriately. For now, just pay attention to your feelings. Watch your behavior and gently guide yourself towards getting to know yourself.

FEELINGS AND FAT

I might be having a perfectly normal day, feeling fine about myself, and then all of a sudden I would start feeling fat. I'd feel really self-conscious, look at myself in a window, and then begin obsessing about how fat I was. The weird thing was that I knew I didn't gain twenty pounds from the moment I woke up to the moment I started feeling fat. But it felt like I did.

— Michelle

What Michelle is experiencing is what we call fat thoughts. Fat thoughts are any thoughts that judge the size and shape of our bodies, such as "My stomach is too fat," "My legs are too big," "My breasts are too small," "My nose is too bumpy." Even though it may feel like these thoughts just pop up into our minds out of nowhere, they usually are a response to some kind of trigger that we are not aware of. Many times the trigger is a certain feeling that we're having.

It's common for women and girls to experience uncomfortable feelings such as shame, embarrassment, anger, frustration, or anxiety, and translate these feelings into fat thoughts because the fat thoughts are more comfortable for them. For example, Michelle was feeling perfectly normal until all of a sudden she felt fat (or had fat thoughts). What happened? Maybe someone made a comment about someone else's body in front of her, so she felt judged and insecure, which translated into her feeling fat. Maybe she got angry with her boyfriend for not calling her, and then thought he didn't like her, which translated into feeling fat. Maybe she was embarrassed in class after not knowing the answer to the question, and so berated herself as fat and stupid. Maybe she was scared about trying out for the soccer team and told herself she was too fat.

There are many reasons why fat thoughts get triggered, and they are different for everyone. In just a few pages we'll do an exercise to help you understand what triggers your fat thoughts.

FEELINGS AND DIETING

The obsession with weight and dieting for me was just as painful as the overeating. Being obsessed with dieting was a way of feeling like my life was going to be okay even when everything else wasn't. I didn't feel anxious about my life because I was too obsessed with dieting. I was not at all conscious of what I was doing.

— Maggie

Like Maggie, many individuals who struggle with food and weight are caught in the ongoing obsession of the diet mentality. We are constantly consumed with counting calories, fat grams, and obeying "diet rules" we have learned in our culture. The actual process of dieting has become so entrenched in our minds that it takes on a life of its own. Trying to stop dieting can be extremely difficult because it also has become a way to cope with uncomfortable feelings.

Diet thoughts are any thoughts that have to do with dieting, such as "I shouldn't eat this, it's too fattening," "I can't eat after 10 P.M. or I'll gain weight," "If I just eat so many fat grams/calories today I'll be good," or "I can't believe she ate that whole bag of chips." Diet thoughts are like fat thoughts. Even though it may feel like these thoughts just pop up into our minds out of nowhere, they usually are a response to some kind of feeling trigger that we are not aware of. Like fat thoughts, you can use your diet thoughts to explore what feelings might have triggered the need to diet or control your food.

Let's look at an exercise to help you figure out what feelings are connected to your fat thoughts and diet thoughts.

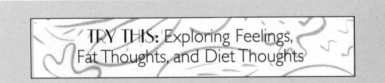

TRY THIS: Exploring Feelings, Fat Thoughts, and Diet Thoughts

1. Whenever you notice yourself having a fat thought or diet thought, stop whatever you are doing and write it down. This may be difficult to do if you are with friends, at a job, or in a classroom. So try to do it on a day when you don't have much going on.
2. Once you've written down the fat/diet thought, think back to what happened right before you had that thought. Where were you? Who were you with? Did someone say something to you? What were you feeling? Close your eyes, if that helps, and try to remember what it was that might have prompted the fat/diet thought.
3. Write down what happened and what you were feeling.

It may be very clear to you, or it may not make any sense. That's okay. It may take time before you understand the link between the feeling and the fat/diet thought. Just continue to write everything down so that you have a journal describing this process.

4. If you can see a direct connection between the feeling and the fat/diet thought, then leave the fat/diet thought behind and focus on the feeling. For example, Michelle realized she was all of a sudden thinking, "I am so fat." She wrote this down, and when she thought about what happened beforehand, she realized that a male friend of hers had made a comment about another girl's body. This made her feel "less than" the other girl and insecure about her looks, which translated into "I'm not as cute as she is, I'm not what boys like, I'm too fat." When she understood this, she realized that it was triggered by her friend's comment and it wasn't really about her being fat — it was about her being uncomfortable having a male friend judging bodies as good or bad. Then Michelle was able to say to herself, "It's not that I'm too fat, it's that I don't like the pressure of my friend judging girls' bodies."

Keep repeating this process when you have a fat or diet thought. Search for the feeling and try to understand how it works. Each time, read over the previous experience and notice if there are similar feelings that come up, or if they are very different. Eventually you will get better at identifying the feelings underneath the fat or diet thoughts, then experiencing the feelings, and letting go of the fat and diet thoughts.

FEELING YOUR FEELINGS

The way I learned to deal with my feelings was to try to change them. "Go out and exercise," my father would say. "It increases your serotonin levels and will make you feel better." So I would. If I were upset, or grumpy, or sick, I'd go exercise. Then I learned that eating would also make me feel better, so I ate. Sometimes I would drink or take pills to change the way I felt. It wasn't until I was in therapy that I realized maybe my feelings were there for a reason and I wasn't supposed to change them.

— Kailey

Feelings are a wise part of us. They are our spirit's way of communicating to us what it is we need. When we feel sad, angry, or anxious, something has happened to cause us distress and it's important to listen to our feelings so we can take care of ourselves. When we feel happy, loving, or excited, something has happened to cause us joy. It is important to listen to these feelings so we can know what we want in our lives. In order to learn from our feelings, we need to be able to feel them and hear what they are telling us about what we need. When we try to change our feelings, we are not learning about our needs.

Eating when we aren't hungry, not eating when we are hungry, and obsessing about food and weight are all ways that we try to change, or cut off, our feelings. As we've seen in the exercises in previous sections, these behaviors come between us and our feelings as a way to protect ourselves from uncomfortable feelings. When we can learn to work through the uncomfortable feelings, we no longer have to depend upon the eating-disorder behaviors to protect us.

Many times it is too scary to explore our feelings by ourselves. Our feelings may overwhelm us or may even lead us to destructive behavior. If this is true for you, you might want to seek the help of a therapist who can help you explore your feelings in a safe way.

You now have worked on identifying your feelings and exploring the relationship between feelings and food, fat thoughts and diet thoughts. The next step is to learn how to process your feelings. Processing feelings means identifying them, expressing them, and taking care of yourself around them. For a while you might experience lots of feelings and still need to overeat, undereat, and obsess. Don't worry, this is normal. It takes a while to learn and trust that you can take care of yourself without these behaviors.

TRY THIS: Feeling Your Feelings

1. When you are aware of feeling any kind of feeling, sit down in a quiet place as soon as possible and be still.
2. Close your eyes, if this is comfortable, and experience your feeling. Let the feeling be as full as possible. Be aware of what is happening inside of your body.
3. Stay with this feeling as long as you can without getting up, without thinking distracting thoughts, without spacing out, without reaching for food. If you find yourself trying to get away from the feeling, just take a breath and bring yourself back to it.
4. If it becomes too scary, that's okay. Let yourself stop, and either come back to it later or find some other type of support (parent, friend, therapist) to help you explore it.
5. Ask yourself, "What am I feeling?" and wait for the answer.
6. Ask yourself if there is any way you need to express this feeling? Can you cry, yell, laugh, draw, punch a pillow, curl up in a ball?

7. Ask yourself what you need right now, in the moment. Your first thought may be something linked to your eating disorder, like food, exercise, or throwing up. But go past these thoughts and try to think of what might meet your feeling needs. Do you need to talk to someone? Do you need a hug? Do you need to tell someone you are angry? Do you need to be alone some more? Do you need to rest? Do you just need to be present with your feelings? What do you want right now? What can you do for yourself to get through this feeling?

8. Stay with yourself for as long as you are comfortable. If you like, take some time to write in a journal about your experience. Don't worry if you have trouble feeling your feelings. Have patience. Each time you do this, it will become easier. After you feel finished, you may still want to eat or exercise or whatever. That's okay. This will shift and change as you learn to trust yourself to feel your feelings.

Showing up for ourselves when we feel horrible is a very difficult task that even many adults have trouble with. Many times as children we didn't get the supportive messages that we needed to hear when we were upset. No matter how much our parents, friends, teachers, or family members love us, there are still many times when they can't give us exactly what we need. This is why we need to learn how to give what we need to ourselves. We sometimes call it "reparenting" ourselves. When we can step in and give ourselves the love and nurturing that we need, we can let go of having to depend on our eating disorder to do it for us.

Once you've been able to have the experience of recognizing your feelings, expressing them, and taking care of yourself around them, you will be able to move more easily throughout the challenges that life brings.

In the Spirit

When I was a teen I worked as hard as I could to be good, look good, get good grades, and to be liked in order to feel secure about myself. I defined who I was by what I did. I didn't realize that there was a very strong part of myself that was unique to me, that had a very important voice with my own truths and passions. As I dealt with the stress of growing up by dieting, binge-ing, and throwing up, my own voice became buried beneath this struggle. I hated my eating disorder, and I hated myself for having it. But now I realize that my eating disorder forced me to look deep within myself. In order to heal, I had to pay attention to this part of myself that was buried beneath years of neglect. My eating disorder was my soul crying out to me to listen.

— Carol

It may seem strange at this point in your life to think that your eating disorder can help you in any way, but we believe it can. We believe that eating disorders are ways of saying, "Help! Something is wrong. Something is amiss. Something is needed!" We believe that at the heart of eating disorders, there is a cry from the deepest part of the soul to be heard. It is a cry to awaken to our true selves, to the essence of who we are.

We, as girls, young women, and old women, are not just bodies to be sculpted into an ideal mold. We are not just stones to be polished into whatever society thinks a woman should be. We are sacred beings. We have, as do all humans, profound and beautiful spirits that guide us every day. In each and every one of us, there is a desire to express who we are in spirit — a desire to play with what makes us unique. Many times this desire gets buried beneath the messages we've received from our culture, families, teachers, or significant people in our lives. Our culture, through advertising, television, and the film industry, feeds us the myth that we will be happy if we reach certain external material goals, such as being thin and pretty, having lots of money, having a nice car, falling in love, or getting married. However, nothing can make us happy unless we have a good relationship with ourselves. When we strive to meet these other external goals, we forget to pay attention to our own unique internal spiritual needs that are waiting to be met.

What Is Spirituality?

When we talk about spirituality, we are not talking about religion. Religions are organized belief systems that people use to express their spirituality. What we are talking about is our own individual relationship to our spiritual self. Our spiritual self is the part of us that holds the blueprint for what we want to create in our lives. It is the source of the energy, ideas, inspiration, and passion that give our lives meaning and purpose. It is the inspiration that takes a seed and changes it into a plant, a bud, and then a rose. Of course it needs light, water, and earth to survive, just as we need food, water, and nurturing to live. But the spiritual self carries the plan that creates the rose itself.

Like the rose in the blooming process, as a teen, you are in the process of finding out who you are in relationship to your friends, family, and teachers. You are beginning to understand what makes you unique as you struggle to fit in, be liked, and accepted. But what makes you unique is not only your body, talents, and personality, but also your spiritual self that holds the potential for what you want to create in life, how you want your life to be, and your desire to express yourself in a way that is yours and yours alone.

As a teenager, you ask yourself, "Where do I belong in this world? What am I doing here? What do I want to be when I grow up?" And many times there is a lot of pressure to have this all figured out before you are ready. But within each of us there are unique truths that are waiting to be expressed. When we are standing in our truth, when we are doing something from a deep internal desire, then what we are doing feels good. It is supported in many ways. It is a powerful force. But many times our truth gets lost. It is hidden among others' expectations of us or our own fears.

Our spiritual self speaks to us through our inner voice. Our inner voice might also be called our wisdom or intuition. Just like listening to our physical wisdom that tells us when we are hungry and when we are full, we can listen to our inner voice that tells us what feeds our soul. When we listen to this voice, we are not only happy, we are also deeply fulfilled on a spiritual level. The deepest core of who we are is satisfied.

When we are caught up in our own world of struggling with food and weight, we forget that we are much more than our eating disorder. We forget that we are much more than our weight, what we just ate, our grades, or our friends. We forget that each and every one of us came from the same source of creation. We were all born with divine spirit. When we start to accept this, just as we accept our bodies and our feelings, we can stop fighting with ourselves and start enjoying ourselves.

In order to recover from an eating disorder, we have to begin to listen to our own internal wisdom about who we are and what we need, not only physically and emotionally, but also spiritually. When we can begin listening to our inner voice, we can start understanding our deepest desires. Here is an exercise to help you get in touch with your spiritual self.

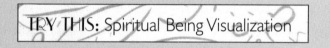

TRY THIS: Spiritual Being Visualization

The following exercise is an imagery exercise. Imagery can be helpful because it allows us to go inside ourselves and find out how we see things. Like any skill, it can take time and practice to work, so be patient. The first few times you do it, you may not get any images. But keep at it and slowly they will become clearer. For some people imagery isn't a useful tool, and if this is true for you, don't worry. Not every method works for everyone.

1. Go to a quiet place and lie or sit down. Take a few deep breaths, breathing in total relaxation and breathing out all tension, just allowing your body to ease into relaxation and peace. Get into a comfortable position and, if you like, close your eyes. Bring your awareness to your breathing. Notice what it feels like to breathe in through your nose, down into your lungs and belly, and back out again. Pay attention to the sensations. Use your breath to bring your awareness into your body and away from your busy mind and all the stresses of the

day. Just notice the natural rhythm of your breathing — don't try to change it. Notice the rising and falling of your belly and chest. Scanning from your head all the way down to your toes, notice if you are holding tension anywhere in your body. Maybe your shoulders are tense, or your belly, or your thighs. Breathe into the tension, imagining that you are sending relaxing oxygen to those areas. As you breathe out, release any tension that you may be holding, allowing your whole body to relax. Let the couch, the floor, or the earth completely support you. There is nothing that you have to hold up. With each breath allow yourself to move deeper into your self, deeper into that place within you where you hold your wisdom, deeper into your own truth.

2. Now visualize your favorite place, knowing that whatever comes up for you is just fine: There is no right or wrong way to do this. You may see the place, or even just sense the place. It may be by the ocean, in a meadow, in the woods. It may even be inside by a fireplace — wherever you feel secure, safe, peaceful, and centered. Take some time to create the mood of this place. Feel the texture, smell the smells, hear the sounds, see the colors and shapes surrounding you. Allow this scene to be as clear as possible.

3. Let yourself sit or lie down in this special place. When you are ready, imagine a wonderful spiritual being coming toward you. Let yourself take as much time as you need to allow this spirit to show itself to you. You may want to walk down a path to look for this being. If so, notice what your path looks like. In the next few

minutes, allow all the time you need for this being to appear.

4. What does this being look like? Take in as many details as possible of this being's physical presence. Notice how she/he carries herself/himself. You may see the being, sense the being, or even hear a voice begin to talk. Sometimes the spiritual self appears not as a person but as a presence, an essence, perhaps experienced by you as pure love. *This is the way that your unconscious chooses to show your spiritual self to you. Let however it comes to you be just fine.*

5. Let this being talk to you and listen to what it has to say. The message may come to you in words, a feeling, or a sensation in your body. Listen carefully. Let whatever message comes sink into all levels of your entire self. Let it nurture and comfort you.

6. Take all the time you need to be with your spiritual being. When you feel finished, you can say good-bye if you like in your own, unique way. Know that you can always come back to your spiritual being whenever you choose to imagine her/him. Now bring your awareness back to your breath, breathing in an awakening and refreshing breath, and breathing out any tension you may be holding. With each breath bring your awareness back into the room, opening your eyes when you are ready. Take a minute to write in your journal whatever you experienced during this imagery.

WHAT IS YOUR SPIRITUAL BELIEF?

We've just told you what we think spirituality is about, and some of it may make sense to you and some of it may not. But what is most important is for you to explore your own beliefs. There are many different beliefs in this world, and most likely you've been exposed to at least a few of them, from parents, friends, or teachers. As you become more independent in your life, it will be important to sort out what makes sense to you and what doesn't. Here is an exercise to help you explore your own personal spiritual beliefs.

TRY THIS: Exploring Spiritual Beliefs

Take out a pen and paper and write down your thoughts, questions, feelings, or anything that comes up in response to these questions. Don't worry about answering them in any "right" way. There is no right answer to these questions. Don't worry if you don't have an answer. These are very difficult questions and for some of them you may not have an answer. Don't worry about your grammar or how you are writing, just write whatever comes to mind. The point is to allow yourself to freely explore whatever thoughts and feelings you have about these questions.

1. Do you believe in God(s), Goddess(es), Great Spirit, Higher Power, Universal Love, Spiritual Presence, or another name you might use?

   A. If yes, what do you imagine this to look like, feel

like, sound like, smell like? What kind of qualities does this have?

    B. If no, what belief system do you have about creation, the source of the universe, or where love comes from?

2. What is the purpose of being alive?
3. What makes you unique in this world?
4. What religious beliefs do you believe are helpful, and what beliefs do you believe are harmful?
5. How, if at all, would you like to expand your spiritual connection?
6. What are your thoughts about prayer?
7. What empowers people and what doesn't?
8. How do you differentiate between what is your truth and what is someone else's?
9. What spiritual experiences have you had in your life? How did they affect you?
10. What experiences have you had in a religious community? How did they affect you?
11. What spiritual needs do you think you might have, and how could you meet these needs?
12. What was it like doing this exercise?

WHAT IS YOUR PASSION?

I wrestled for high school and that is like a totally demanding sport. Unlike every other sport where you need to be small, I had to be big. Having to change back and forth was very trying. Then having to be okay with the fact that I had to wear spandex with legs this long. That was very hard for me to do, because I couldn't be comfortable with myself when I was in front of people on the mat. I didn't even think about trying to accept it. I just kind of had to get over it or else I wasn't going to be able to perform this sport very well. And it was some-thing I was enjoying too much to give up on just because I was uncom-fortable with the way I looked. I didn't change in any size but to me I felt like I did just because I didn't worry any more. I wasn't worried about whether I was happy with this weight. This was the weight I had to be. It was like a total pressure off my shoulders. I could stomp and kill. It was awesome for me. To just get over the fact that I felt like I needed to be different than how I was. I finally learned to just be cool with the way I was. I was totally happy and at peace.

— Jenniffer

When Jenniffer realized that in order to do her sport she had to get over her desire to have a smaller body, she stepped into her passion. She had found something she loved to do and she found out that she could do it well. She was confronted on a lot of dif-ferent levels about how her body looked, in Spandex, and in front of a lot of people. But, as she let the negative messages about her body go, she was able to hear what her body and her spirit were telling her to do. She loved wrestling, and through her love for her sport, she came to love her body. She found her creative self and in so doing, she found happiness and peace.

This is a beautiful example of how, when you are living your dream, your desire, and your passion, your obsession with food and weight is not that important anymore. Recovery comes when you know what you want and you become willing to do it, even if it takes just "getting over yourself."

It is not unusual for many girls in this culture to be bored or depressed with their lives. Many girls feel that they are trapped in a cage. Societal pressures to be safe, sweet, pretty, thin, or sexy prevent them from living up to, or even knowing, their true poten-tial. They are not given many positive role models of women who live their passions. They are more likely to see women who are constantly worried about what they look like, instead of *who* they are. However, positive role models are there. You just need to look for them. Many women are completely in love with their work. You can see it in their faces and in their work. These are women who listen to a different drummer — themselves.

The most important thing now is to find your own creative passionate wants, desires, and dreams. Then you must dare to follow them. You can if you will let yourself.

TRY THIS: Exploring Your Creativity

1. Find a safe place to go where you won't be disturbed for a few hours. Bring some paper, some colored pencils or pens, and your imagination.
2. Close your eyes and let yourself drift into your subconscious mind. Remember, this is like dreaming, but you are still awake.
3. Take some long deep breaths and relax. As you breathe in and out, release any tension you might be holding in your body. With each breath, let yourself move deeper and deeper into the place within you where you hold all of your creative energy.
4. Let yourself remember a time when you felt you were in touch with your creative self. This might have been a long time ago when you were a little girl. See if you can picture yourself being creative. It doesn't matter how or with what, just take what comes. It could be anything: finger painting, sculpting with Play-Doh™, or writing poetry. Or maybe you are dancing or acting

in a play that you made up. Maybe you are playing with dolls or objects and making them come to life in your imagination. It doesn't matter what the activity was, as long as you were completely engrossed and lost in it.

5. Notice how old you were. What were you wearing? Who was there with you? What were you creating? What colors and smells were there? What were you feeling as you were doing these things?

6. Now as you continue to watch yourself in your own creative endeavors, slowly grow yourself up. Notice if there is any point at which you stopped yourself, or anyone else stopped you, from being creative. How old were you? What happened? What messages did you receive? Were they positive or negative? See if you can pinpoint exactly what happened, if anything, to your creative self.

7. Now see if you can change any of the messages by creating new ones that are positive and supportive. Is there anything you need to say or give to your inner child that would allow you to find and express your creative self more fully and more often? Imagine giving this to yourself.

8. Now visualize yourself as a creative being. Let yourself be fully in your body and your imagination. What does this feel like? What could you create if you were really and truly able to be here? Let the images flow and dance across your mind's eye. Let yourself see all the pictures you could paint, all the poems you could write, all the dances you could dance, all the sports you could play, all the wonderful things that you could do, and more. Let them fill you up completely.

9. When you are ready, open your eyes and get out your paper and pencils. Write or draw whatever came up for you in this exercise.

10. Look at your schedule and see if you can set aside some times during the week to start living your passions and your dreams. Let yourself see and know what is in your imagination. Realize that these are your gifts to yourself and to the world.

WHAT ARE YOUR GIFTS?

I became a peer educator because I wanted to fight against body hatred. I had spent so much of my life obsessing about what I had for lunch and whether or not I had exercised that day. It was so time consuming and it just ate away at me. When I finally realized that I didn't have to live my life like that anymore, I wanted to tell other girls that they didn't have to spend their lives like that anymore, either.

— Vanessa

Vanessa has found her calling. It might not be the only one she ever has, but it is something that she has experience with and that she's good at. It's also something that she has total passion for. The body hatred that had consumed her in her own past helps her connect with other girls. That connection, in turn, helps the other girls. One of the beautiful things about Vanessa's story is that she took something that had caused her great pain in the past and turned it around to use for healing in the future. This is one of the many gifts that recovery can bring to us.

All of us came into this world with a special calling. Your calling is something you were called to do by divine plan, something that no one else can do the same way that you can do it. This is what we mean when we talk about the gifts that you give to yourself and to the world. Every one of us has them. They are what makes us not only human, but also divine. The world is a better place because of each person and the gift each person is sharing with us. There are gifts that bring beauty to our eyes and our ears. Maybe we are emotionally moved by something someone wrote, danced, or played as an expression of their creative gift. Or sometimes the gift is simply the special feeling we have when we are with certain people, because of how they are with us. Realize that you have a gift too. This gift is your spiritual calling. Your challenge is to let yourself find it, express it, and live it.

If your life has been about how you look and what you did or did not eat, it might be hard to believe that there can be anything else. But you are so much more than your size or what you eat. When the obsession is gone, what is left is you and your creative self. This is a very powerful place to be. From this place you can do anything you can dream of; anything is possible. The small voice within can be heard so much better without the running negative commentary of your obsessive thoughts about your weight, your food, or what you should or should not look like. Imagine what your life would have been like if you had been living your creative, spiritual path all this time.

The way I got over my bulimia was by taking a dance class that was about how good you could feel in your body, not about how good you would look in your body. This put me in touch with how much my body loves to move and I feel so awesome when I'm dancing and moving. Next year I'm going to start dancing professionally and one day I hope to make my living by doing what I love.

— Kellie

Kellie discovered the value of finding what you love to do. Little by little, you need to let go of the desire to change your body or its shape and, instead, listen to the voice within that will guide you toward your true desires. This may mean "coming out of the closet" about what you have not been willing to share before. Maybe you've always wanted to paint but you've been scared to admit it. Or maybe you want to sing, dance, write, or work on cars, but you don't think others will approve.

The first step is to get clear on what it is that you want to do and where your own unique talents lie. The next exercise can help you to become clear on at least what you might want to do with them. Then you can make decisions on what to do from there.

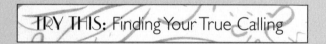

TRY THIS: Finding Your True Calling

1. Find a nice place to sit down, close your eyes, and get comfortable. Breathe deeply and naturally. Let go of all tensions of the day and let yourself relax.
2. Go to the place within that you know is the "safe place" for you. Spend a few moments here just *being*. Feel how this place feels to you. Smell the smells of this place. Hear the sounds of this place and see the colors of this place.
3. Imagine a giant movie screen in front of you. Let the image of yourself in your present, everyday life come up on the screen. See what it is that you usually do everyday. Don't get attached to any of it. Just let it float across the screen and fade out.
4. Now, let the image of you as a little girl come up. What were your hopes and dreams for yourself? Keep letting

the images come, no matter what they are. What were your dreams? Did you want to be a doctor? A mom? A businessperson? A shopkeeper? A computer analyst? An engineer? A painter? A dancer? Maybe none of these things and maybe all of these things. Just let the images float across the screen and fade out.

5. Now see yourself at the age you are now, but let yourself imagine these little-girl hopes and dreams from your more mature perspective. Try each one on for size. Imagine yourself doing any of these things. How does it feel? Does it fit? Is it what you really want to do? Or do you want to do something that you haven't even thought of yet? Just relax and let the images come to you and, as they do, try them on for size and see if they make you happy.

6. If you are doing something else in your life that does not make you happy, see if in your imagination you can let go of it. Then try something else on. Don't worry if you don't know how any of this is going to happen. What you are doing is exploring your true calling. The way to pursue it will be made clearer later.

7. Imagine yourself really doing your dream. Really see it, smell it, hear it, and live it for a few moments.

8. If it doesn't feel right, let it go and let yourself try on another one. Take as long as you need to be really clear about what feels best deep inside of you.

9. When you have found the images that feel right, just let them fade off the movie screen. Come back to yourself in the present. Let yourself breathe and take all that you were shown deep within you. Just stay with this for a moment or two.

10. Open your eyes slowly and come back to the room.
11. Write down in your journal any insight you have had about what your true calling might be. As much as possible in the next few days or weeks, start to open up to the possibility of following your true calling.

WHEN BAD THINGS HAPPEN

When I was in middle school my close girlfriend died of cancer. I didn't know it then, but now I realize it threw me into a spiritual crisis. I tried to make sense of it, but of course I couldn't. Where was God in all of this? What kind of life had I signed up for, where good people died and their family was left devastated by it? It made no sense. I think a big hole was blown through my security that life was safe. I think at some point I abandoned whatever faith I had in the world, in the Great Spirit, and in myself.

— Carol

Sometimes "bad" or frightful things happen in our lives that have long-lasting, traumatic effects. When family or friends die or become dangerously sick, it can have a huge impact on our relationship to the world. If we've been hurt by someone — sexually, physically, verbally, or emotionally — our relationship to ourselves and the world can become severely damaged. Divorce, drug or alcohol abuse, or eating disorders among family members can be harmful as well. Even witnessing a trauma that occurs to someone else, such as a car accident, people fighting, or inappropriate touching, can affect how we view the world.

If something like this has happened to you, it's important to explore how this might have affected your beliefs about the world and spirituality. Sometimes our experiences keep us from trusting that anything good could happen to us, or that we are even worthy of being loved. Sometimes, especially if the event occurred when we were young, we might even feel responsible for it, as if it were our fault. Getting professional help from a therapist or talking to a trusted parent or friend can help you sort out how this traumatic event shaped your view of the world. Then you can decide how this view helps or hinders you in your life and make choices about what you want to change.

Often, even though we can't change a certain situation, we can change our attitude about it. Even in the most difficult situations, we can find something that brings us love and learning.

Where Is Your Faith?

If there is one thing I want to say to all of the girls out there who are struggling with this issue, it is this: Have faith and don't worry because you're gonna be fine. We're in this together and I know that we can get through it together. I am free of body hatred and I am freeing you now of any body hatred that you have. It's just not worth it. It brings you to a lower place. Think about all the wonderful things you could be doing if you were not worrying about your body. There's a whole world out there and a lot of inspiring things to embark on. I just want you to think about that and know that you are going to make it through this.

— Maggie

If you feel like you are all alone and no one will ever understand the way you feel about your body or your food, remember that all of the girls whose stories are woven throughout this book know what you are going through. They have gone through it too. When you are in pain and confusion about having an eating disorder, it's easy to think that this is how it always will be. But like Maggie said, you will make it through this. And the way you will make it through is allowing yourself to have faith that you are connected to a much bigger source of love, one that will guide you, take care of you, and inspire you.

To have faith is to trust. Give yourself the gift of trusting that there is a divine purpose for your life. Open to the small voice within that will be there for your whole life long. This, the voice of your higher power, is connected to the entire universe and will always hold you in love.

When you are stuck in the voice of your eating disorder, you are stuck in pain, fear, isolation, control, and obsession. If you allow yourself to go beneath the eating disorder, to find out what you are really trying to say to yourself, then you are listening to a much more loving voice. Below the eating disorder is the voice of your own soul. You can learn to listen to this voice when you are wondering what to do next.

The recovery process is a long and winding road that starts deep within yourself and, with many twists and turns, always leads you back to yourself. Trust this road and trust yourself. You have this disorder for a really good reason. This is the way you have learned to get your own attention. Your obsession, your overeating, or your undereating is telling you something. Have faith, let go, and surrender to the process of discovering what you are really trying to say.

Many, many girls and women who have come through Beyond Hunger were at their wit's end about how to get over their obsession with food and weight. But the sooner they could trust and have faith that a loving source was there for them and they didn't have to do it alone, the sooner they got better. Letting go allows you to rest, breathe, and be still. When you are holding on tightly, it's hard to hear anything but the critical and fearful chatter of your mind. When you can let go, you begin to hear the loving spiritual guidance from your own soul. The next exercise is designed to help you do this.

TRY THIS: Exploring Faith

1. When you find yourself struggling with yourself or your eating disorder, stop whatever you're doing, go to a place where you can be alone, sit down, and breathe.
2. As you breathe, try for a moment to let go of the struggle with your feelings.
3. Ask your higher power and/or spiritual self to be with you. Imagine being supported in whatever way you need.
4. Imagine that you are placing your struggle in the hands of your higher power or spiritual self.
5. Get up and go back to whatever you were doing, even if it was bingeing, purging, or starving, but do it with the awareness that there is a very loving, caring source present with you, holding on to your struggle for you.
6. Notice how it feels to live without having to hold on to the struggle, knowing that it's being held by a much bigger presence than just yourself.
7. Notice what happens as you walk through the same old behaviors with a new awareness of this presence.
8. Continue to do the exercise whenever any type of struggle comes up, whether it be with food, your weight, obsessive thoughts, relationships, or any other type of problems you might have.

By letting go of your struggles and trusting that your higher self will help you with anything that might come your way, you start to reclaim your spiritual self. This allows you to awaken to your own divinity which, in turn, heals the wounds that eating disorders carry: separation from body, mind, and spirit. As you go through the process of defining for yourself what your spiritual self needs and wants, you begin a transformation that will take you far beyond the struggle with food and weight.

When you look into the mirror and see your whole self, not just your body or your body parts, you open up to the teaching of your own soul. When you look into the mirror and see your true spirit, the mirror will reflect back to you what your soul has to say; that you are not alone, that you are loved, and that you are a valuable sacred being. When you see and hear this over and over again, you will look at others through the eyes of compassion, and with respect for their own unique spirits, too.

In this way your transformation is not only about healing for yourself and your eating disorder. It is about healing for the world. This is a true spiritual transformation, and this is true recovery.

Tell It Like It Is

When I took a stand to love my body and be out there, it was really hard because I was afraid that there would be people bashing me. But it was okay. I felt so completely in my body. I felt it through all inches of my body so I knew I was right. Now I don't have time to be smooshed anymore. I don't. And even though it took a lot of patience, I continued to put myself out there. Now the people around me are almost like on their knees. They can't believe how precious I have become since the time I felt like shit about myself.

— Maggie

When you start to "tell it like it is" you start to speak and live your truth. Speaking your truth means communicating to others your genuine feelings, beliefs, and needs. Living your truth is putting into action what your own heart and soul desires. Sometimes it is hard or scary to speak and live our truth. As girls and women, we have been brought up to worry about *how we look* instead of knowing *who we are*. We have been trained to be passive instead of proactive. We have been encouraged to take care of others before we take care of ourselves.

It is a challenging and radical step for any female to stop obsessing about how she looks and to step into the power of who she is. It is especially challenging, however, if you are a girl with an eating disorder. You have to stop dieting, stop obsessing, stop counting fat grams, stop worrying about what size and shape you are. You have to learn how to say, "No, I'm not going to live like that," to a culture that makes its money out of keeping you sick. As you are continually bombarded with messages by the media and society, you have to continue to bring yourself back to remembering what is most important to you.

It is also difficult to find a way to talk to your friends and family without diet talk. This can be really lonely. Often this is the only language you have ever spoken with your girlfriends, and the result may be that at first you don't know what else to talk about. But eventually you will start to talk about other things, like who you really are, what you really think, and where you are going with your life.

This is why it is so important to find others on your path: people who will understand you and support you while you are doing this work within yourself. You need people who will walk with you through the fear and resistance of others and keep you steady on the journey. This journey is for the everyday girl who is born with the right to live her truth no matter what that truth is. There are millions of girls and women out there who are like you and who are walking paths similar to yours. Many of them have gone before you and can turn back and help you come forward. Many of them are behind and need your help to come up to where you are. Remember, we are all in this together, and you don't have to do this alone.

When you find yourself speaking or living your truth, it may be difficult for some people to understand it or accept it. Some people might not be ready to hear. They might resist. They may lash out at you with discouraging words or actions. This is called a "backlash." It may come from your family, your friends, your teachers, or even from within yourselves. But wherever it comes from, it is usually an expression of fear, fear of the unknown, the uncontrolled, the radical, or the painful. You might have to stand up for your truth again and again. Be patient. As you get better about taking care of yourself, living your own life, meeting your own needs, expressing your true self, the people around you will reflect what is in your heart back out to you.

JUST SAY "NO," IF THAT'S WHAT YOU WANT TO SAY

I was talking to a girlfriend of mine who is really popular with the guys. They are always asking her out. She was telling me how some old, creepy guy had asked her out. I asked her how she responded. She said she told him, "No, thanks." "That's it?" I asked. "No, thanks?" She looked at me kind of funny and said, "Yeah, that's it. 'No, thanks.' That's all I ever say." I was shocked. It had never occurred to me that it could be that simple and that easy to say no to someone. I always thought I had to explain my "no" to people so they would understand or so I wouldn't hurt their feelings. I thought of all the messes I got myself into because I didn't know how to say no. What freedom to know all I had to say was "no, thanks" to anybody about anything — no explanation necessary.

— Ann

You may not believe it, but you have a right to say no. Learning to say no is a crucial step in this recovery, mainly because women and girls have not been taught how to say it. However, everyone has the right to say no. It is time to take back that right.

It requires a level of self-esteem that you may not have yet, but can learn. You are building your self-esteem every time you listen to the call of your own needs and take care of yourself. The first thing to realize is that for many years it has been someone else's job to take care of you. But now it is getting near the time that you will be taking care of yourself. This is a transition that everyone goes through. The transition can be rough. The more you can stay connected with your truth and be honest and open, the easier it will be.

Saying no may be difficult when you feel pressured by friends to do something you don't want to do. You may even be confused about what you want, so you just go along with what everyone else is doing. The first step in saying no is getting clear about what you are feeling and what you need in a certain situation. If you find that you don't want to do something, then you can ask yourself if you feel comfortable saying no. If not, look at what you fear. Are you afraid someone won't like you, or will be mad at you, or will talk about you behind your back? Talk to someone who may be able to support you. With parents, teachers, or other authority figures, you might say no and still have to do something. In these situations, the adults should be keeping the best interests of everyone in mind. Even though you may still have to do something you disagree with, at least you will have expressed how you felt about it.

Here is an exercise to help you feel comfortable saying no.

TRY THIS: Saying No

1. Find a friend or someone who will work with you on this. Make sure it is someone who understands what you are doing and will support you in learning how to say no.

2. Make a commitment to say no to her once a day for a week. No matter what she asks you to do, say no. Have her call you and ask you to do something. Say no every time. Start with small requests and work up to bigger ones. For example:

"No, I can't babysit tonight."

"No, I can't help you with your homework today."

"No, I don't want to go with you to the movies."

"No, I'm not going to call that guy for you."

"No, I don't want to talk about food or weight with you."

"No, you can't drive my car."

"No, I don't want to go to the store for you."

3. As you say no this week, pay attention to what comes up for you each time you say it. Do you feel selfish? Guilty? Powerful? Not nice? Relieved? Grown-up? Mean? Lonely? In control? Frightened or insecure? Sure of yourself? Taken care of? Write down in your journal what happens to you inside every time you say no. Also notice how often you say no to yourself, and ask yourself why. Write that down, too. Do you want to give her all sorts of reasons why you are not going to do something? This is unnecessary. A simple no is all that is required. If you'd like to explain why, try to communicate the simple truth instead of making up excuses.

4. The second week, have your friend start saying no to you. How does it feel to be on the other side of someone setting boundaries? Do you feel resentful or glad that she is taking care of herself? If different or conflicting messages come up for you, acknowledge them and talk about them with someone or write them in your journal.

> 5. In the third week do not say yes to anything that you really do not want to do. This takes a lot of soul searching. It also requires making a real commitment to take care of your *whole* self. Make choices about what is truly the best thing for you to do in the long run.

Eventually, as you keep learning how to say no, you will learn the power of saying yes. When you are truly making choices, and not always doing things you don't want to do, you have time to do the things that your heart desires. When you learn the power of saying no, you learn the power of saying yes.

I gave myself exercise when I felt like it. I ate when I wanted. I stopped being so restrictive. I found a balance for myself and what my body wanted.

— Maggie

Maggie found that what she needed was balance. This is a common theme. Sometimes, especially for girls and women, it's hard to find the right balance, not only in eating or exercising, but in everything else in our lives. How do we balance school or work with our own downtime? How do we balance time with our friends, family, and lovers? How do we balance our time for others with time we want for ourselves? How do we balance our duties with our own creative endeavors? This is a tall order, but it can be accomplished by learning how to set limits and boundaries in your life. The first thing to remember is that you have a right to come *first* in your life.

When you come *first,* you don't have to struggle for your own time. It will be there for you. It is easier to live in the abundance of time rather than in deprivation. Remind yourself that you can always choose. You can learn to choose what you want every moment. You can learn to set limits and boundaries. The following exercise can help you do this.

TRY THIS: Setting Limits and Boundaries

1. Pick a day when not much is going on. Promise yourself that today, as much as you can, you will really listen to what you want to do, instead of what you should do. When you hear the call for what you want, acknowledge that, and give yourself what you need.

2. When you have a question about what to do, breathe, get centered, and ask yourself what it is you want to do. What is true for you in the moment? Listen to your inner voice.

3. What might come up is all the things that you *should* do instead of the things you *want* to do. These two things don't have to fight. Just let yourself figure out the best thing to do, taking into consideration all the ways that you can juggle your needs, desires, and responsibilities. Notice the feeling in your body as you sort through all the different ways that you can spend your time.

4. If you find yourself doing something that doesn't feel good in your body — overeating, overspending, overworking, or just doing more than you really want to do — stop. Notice what happens to you when you just stop.

5. Let yourself explore the many reasons why you would do something that doesn't feel good. Trust yourself to

know what is the best thing for you to do next, and then let yourself do it.

Take it slow, this is a process. You are just practicing setting limits. You are learning how to set boundaries, not only with yourself, but also with the others around you.

THE POWER OF YOUR OWN VOICE

I realized that the negative messages inside my head are other people's thoughts that I have made into mine. Now I just push them away and think about what my body individually wants and needs. I focus on that 'cause it's different than anyone else's. It has totally opened my eyes and made me a lot more accepting.

— Kristian

Finding your own voice beneath all the messages of others can be very hard and might take a long time. It takes patience and time to sort through. But as Kristian said, the thing to remember is to come back to your body and to your own truth.

Sometimes when I look at my body, I hear that voice in the background saying that if I'm not hungry one day then it's good because maybe I'll lose some weight. But I think, "Hey, that's society." But I guess I feel that it's about healing myself. As much as I want to believe that I am doing this work, and accepting myself, and listening to my body, and doing all that, there's that voice that really describes the media mentality and not this mentality. And so I get angry at myself because I'm scared that I'm not strong enough to do it, to do this work and really recover. It just irritates me. I'm frustrated. Why can't I just do it and be fine? I'm listening to my body. I'm doing all that and this voice comes up. Why is it there? The diet mentality itself is so annoying and so obsessed and crazed that to have that voice within me seems so incredible.

— Kate

The voices of the diet mentality and society are incredibly strong and powerful. It is confusing and frustrating to work and work through this issue and find that sometimes it is still there within us. But as Kate said, it is about healing. And healing takes time. Especially when the society you live in is unhealthy.

Finding your own voice beneath the layers of others means going through all of the many different messages you have been taught and coming up with what will best serve you. Each time you hear these conflicting messages or voices in your head, ask yourself, "Does it help me to believe this? Is this a supportive message or does it make me feel bad about myself or my body?"

Another way to find your own voice is to learn how to express yourself to others about what is true for you. For instance, you might find that you don't want to be around an old friend because she drives you crazy with her diet mentality. It might help to give her this book so that she knows what you are going through. Some people may never understand. And these people might just have to leave your life.

Recovery changes your whole life, not just your eating habits or your body. So it stands to reason that the relationships in your life change as well. Every different person who goes through this recovery experiences a different reaction from her friends and family. That is why it is important to find someone who can be there for you while you go through all the ups and downs of your own stuff and the stuff of others.

The next exercise is designed to help you know your own truth, and say what you need to say.

TRY THIS: Expressing Your Truth

1. Take a few moments to breathe, and scan your body. Release any tension that you might be holding.
2. Get in touch with something that you feel you need to express to someone. Is there something you've been wanting to say, but haven't been able to? Is there something you want to share with someone, but don't know how? Don't worry about talking face-to-face with the person. You don't have to! The important thing is to get in touch with what you would like to say if you could.
3. Now open your eyes and write down all that you would like to say. Don't edit anything. Just let the words flow. Let out all your thoughts and feelings on the paper. When a strong feeling comes up, underline what you were writing and then move on.
4. When you are done, go back and read through it. When you reach the parts that are underlined, try to go to the feeling and experience it as fully as possible. Notice how it feels to be experiencing it now. See if the child within you needs something from the part of you that can be nurturing and loving. Then, see if you can give to yourself whatever you need. Repeat this in each part of the letter that strong feelings came up for you.
5. Now go back and read it again. If you want to change it, go ahead. Notice how it felt to truly express your self. Leave it for now and, at another time, come back

to it and see if there are any changes. When it feels finished, you may want to share what you came up with — or you may not. You may want to write another letter to a specific person, or just a general one to society at large. Whatever you want to do is okay. What is important is that you know the truth for yourself and you were able to express it. This is a powerful start!

BEING HEARD

When I try to talk to my parents or friends about my eating disorder, they just don't understand. I know they are trying, but I can tell by what they say that they don't have a clue. If I really told my parents what I was doing, they would freak out and start watching me every second. My friends also become really worried and start telling me I should eat and stuff. I know they are trying to help but it just makes me feel more alone and ashamed, like I should be able to just stop doing this. And when I know they are worried about me, I just try to hide it from them so they won't know what I'm doing.

— Peggy

Struggling with food and weight can be a lonely experience. Even if you have friends or family who listen to you, they may not be able to relate to what you are saying. Sometimes they may even react to what you're saying with their own fears, which makes it even more difficult to talk to them. You may have friends who are struggling with food and weight who understand what you are talking about. This might be helpful, but unless they have experienced some healing themselves they may have difficulty supporting you in your healing process.

As you begin to listen to your own voice, it's important to

have someone in your life who can listen to you respectfully. It's not helpful when someone makes fun of your ideas, makes you feel like they are dumb or stupid, or is not interested in listening to you. When someone listens to you respectfully, they let you talk without interrupting. They are genuinely interested in what you have to say, and they don't belittle your thoughts or feelings. They may have a different opinion, but they can express it without saying your opinion is dumb or stupid.

Sometimes finding a person who will listen is hard. You may need to test out a number of different friends and adults to see if they can do this for you. Most schools have counselors who are available to talk. A school nurse may be able to help you find someone. There are many therapists who specialize in the treatment of eating disorders who can also help. There may be eating and body-image support groups in your area that are facilitated by a qualified professional. Support groups can help decrease isolation and provide a safe place for you to talk about your struggles with other teens who understand. The most important thing is to take the risk to communicate to someone you trust that you need someone you can talk to about this. And then make sure that the person you find feels safe to you and is helpful to you.

If you feel too vulnerable to tell someone your thoughts or feelings, writing in a journal is a very safe way to express them. This can help you sort out what they are. Then, as you read them over, you will get to know your own voice. Here is a journal exercise to help you listen to your own thoughts and feelings.

TRY THIS: Finding Your Voice in Your Journal

Buy a journal, if you don't already have one, or just start with sheets of paper that you can keep in a safe place.

Begin by writing whatever comes to mind. It doesn't have to be full sentences or grammatically correct. It doesn't have to be sweet and nice. It doesn't even have to make sense! Just write whatever you are thinking or feeling. If you get stuck, close your eyes. Take a few deep breaths and just listen to your body and your thoughts. If you get an image, write about that image. Let go of any rules you have about what or how you should be writing. Just write.

Write until you are ready to stop. When you like, either now or at a later time, look over what you've written and listen to what you have said. Do you have any thoughts or feelings? If so, write these down. If you find yourself judging what you have written, stop yourself. Try to listen respectfully. Notice if there is anything you've written that you feel like sharing with anyone. If so, can you think of someone trustworthy you would like to tell? If not, that's fine. If so, maybe you can find a time to sit down with that person and talk to them.

Standing Out

When I went to my twenty-year high school reunion I was afraid that everyone there had read our book It's Not about Food, knew that I was bulimic, and was horrified. Even though my close friends from high school reassured me that they loved me and respected me, I still felt very vulnerable. After all, this was high school where all of my dieting, bingeing, and insecurities started. Even though I was thirty-eight years old, in a heartbeat, I was feeling sixteen again. I went anyway and, actually, no one had even read my book, so it wasn't an issue. But I was amazed at how vulnerable it felt to have my secret told. Writing our book was a risk I had to take. It became clear to me that using my voice and speaking my truth were more important to me than what other people thought of me.

— Carol

There comes a time when speaking our truth becomes more important than what other people think of us. Unfortunately many of us weren't raised this way. But when your life is compromised by struggles with food and weight, it's an absolute necessity to start using your voice instead of your body to speak.

There are many pressures teenagers feel to do things in order to fit in and be liked. It's not unusual for young girls to go along with having sex, even if they don't want to. Peer pressure has influenced many young girls to start smoking, drinking, or taking drugs, even if they prefer not to. Some start hiding their abilities in school or sports because they are afraid of being teased as the "nerd" or "super jock." The risk of being different and standing out is too unbearable. Why is it so unbearable?

When our self-esteem is so low that we depend upon others to feel good about ourselves, it can be scary to stand out or risk being judged. Yet when we can't say what we believe in and stand in our truth, we compromise ourselves and we never get what we need to take care of ourselves. It is a difficult choice to make, especially at such a vulnerable time in our lives.

When you come to a crossroads and feel there is a conflict between your truth and what is expected of you, it might be helpful to find supportive people to talk to. They may be able to help you find a way to communicate to your friends or family, or to cope with judgments that may come up from others. You may find that in some situations it is just not safe, and you have to wait until the situation changes or you feel more able to handle it. Again, you can always seek professional help if it becomes too overwhelming to deal with by yourself. You may become so passionate about your truth that you need to become politically active, by joining an organization, public speaking, changing a law, or changing something in your community. Everyone is different. You will know what it is that you want and need by listening to your own voice. Here is an exercise to help you look at taking a stance.

TRY THIS: Taking a Stance

Think of some situation in your life where you feel like you are not being true to yourself. Can you think of a time when you did something that you really didn't want to? Can you think of something you really want to do or say, but are too afraid? Can you think of a situation in which you felt pressured by peers to be a certain way, or do a certain thing? Take this situation, and write it down. Answer the following questions:

1. What is your truth in this situation? What do you really want to say or do?
2. What is keeping you from being in your truth? What are you afraid will happen?
3. Will being in your truth put you at risk for physical or emotional harm?
   A. If yes, with whom can you discuss this situation to help you take care of yourself in the future?
   B. If no, how can you find support, within yourself or from others, to help you do what you feel is right to do the next time you're in this kind of situation?

Setting limits, saying no, finding your own voice, and speaking and living your truth are challenging for everyone. Most adults still struggle with how to do this in their daily lives. Like any challenge, it becomes easier with practice. As you learn to respect your own truth, you will also learn to respect others. We all have different ways of being in this world. Yours may be very different from your parents or friends, but that doesn't make you — or them — right or wrong. Living in harmony requires respect for each other's unique truth. When we can embrace each other's truth, then we can work toward finding agreements that honor all sides.

As you begin to respect the wisdom of your body, emotions, and spirit, your truth will be able to blossom. We will all be blessed by it.

CELEBRATING DIVERSITY

I grew up in the Phillipines and there thin people are the people that they bash all the time because it is beautiful to be fat. The people in the media and everything are fat and it's "beautiful." I think it represents your wealth and your health to be fat. So to me the pressure was always to be fat because that was beautiful. Everybody was like, "You want to look like this movie star," and she is very fat compared to the models here. Ever since I was little they told me that. And then when I moved here last year my Grandma was like, "Oh my Gosh, look at you, you have to get thin, you have to get thin!" And my friends and stuff, they're always wanting to be thin. And then I don't know what is beautiful anymore because I know it's just a cultural thing. The pressure there was way different than it was here. There it was always you need to gain weight and here it was you need to lose weight and obviously I can't live in the middle. That would be the ocean!

— Candice

Every culture has its own definition of beauty, and they can be very different. Candice talks about finding herself caught between two distinct standards of beauty: one from her own ethnic background and one from the country where she is living now. This is not unusual. A study done on Chinese university students in the United States showed that the more Chinese females became a part of this culture, the more eating-disorder symptoms they had.[1] This suggests that as individuals from other cultures integrate into ours, the dominant culture, they will experience more of these dominant cultural pressures to diet and be thin. A study done in Fiji, an island where the traditional definitions of beauty did not include thinness, showed that within two years of the introduction of American television, young women expressed the desire to be thinner.[2] The influence of the media was so strong that a culture's entire perspective of what is beautiful was changed in two years!

The media tries to tell you what the perfect person is supposed to look like. The Mexicans are supposed to have long, dark, curly hair and have a little chola look, black people are supposed to have big breasts and big bottoms, and white people are supposed to be tall and skinny with blonde hair.

— Lilia

Even within different ethnic groups, many young girls feel there is a stereotypical way they should look. They may feel pressure from family members, relatives, and friends to look one way, and then feel pressure from peers and the culture to look another way.

I think sometimes African American women are given a very double standard because we're taught from day one, you know, be proud, be a beautiful black sister. But then again, if you look

*at the ads, you see these models with the very light green eyes,
and the blond hair, and it's long, and they're tiny, and it's like
they're showing you a black woman almost looking like a white
woman.*

— La Tanya

Like La Tanya, many young girls find that, although their families are giving them one message, they still feel the pressure of the
media to be another way. Studies show that black women have a
lower rate of restrictive eating disorders, such as anorexia, but that
as they become part of the mainstream culture, the rate increases.
This may be because they buy into the dominant culture's definition of beauty more.

It's very confusing to deal with so many different messages
when you're in the process of figuring out who you are and what
you want to be. Maybe your family thinks one thing, your peers
think another, and the culture you live in thinks yet another. The
different messages you get tell you not only what you should look
like, but how you should act, what role you should play in your
culture, what careers are valued, and what foods to eat. Who do
you end up listening to?

Individuals who have a race, gender, religion, sexual preference, handicap, certain body type, or any other quality that is in
the minority, suffer from being treated as "different" and "less
than" and unequal. It's no secret that our culture still holds
many prejudices that are being acted out with violence and
aggression. Part of recovering from an eating disorder is learning to respect and celebrate our own and each other's differences. This means exploring the judgments we make about these
differences.

As we've said before, it's very important to be able to sort out
which messages are helpful to you and which are hurtful. Here is

an exercise to look at your own uniqueness, the judgments you make, where they came from, and what you choose to believe.

TRY THIS: Exploring What Makes You Unique

1. Make a list of all of the unique qualities about your body and yourself.
2. After each of these qualities, write down your judgment of it, good or bad.
3. Next to each judgment, write down where you think it comes from: your family, your relatives, your ethnic culture, the media, your peers, a teacher, or anyone else.
4. Finally, write down what you yourself believe about these unique qualities. If you find certain qualities that you don't like because they are different, see if you can learn to understand them and develop respect for where they came from.
5. Find someone who you can trust to talk to about ways in which you feel different from the mainstream culture. If there are ways you are being treated unfairly because of a difference, see if there is a safe adult who might be able to help you.

Finding out who you are as a unique individual is part of becoming an adult. Unfortunately, many adults never learn to fully appreciate their own and others' differences. We get so caught up in feeling insecure that we make the differences into issues of right or wrong and good or bad. But when we learn to feel secure with ourselves and our own uniqueness, we have room to love and respect others for theirs.

ACTIVISM

When you take your beliefs and put them into action, the world spins. Our culture grows and changes through individuals becoming active in the community. There are many ways to take what you have learned from your eating disorder and make a difference in the lives of others. We have been blessed to watch young women take all kinds of action, from writing a letter to being a peer educator, and have seen the profound impact they have had on others. Activism also helps to reinforce what you have already learned. If you find yourself ready to take action but don't know what to do, check out our Resource List.

NOTES

[1] Katzman, Davis C., "Perfection as Acculturation: Psychological Correlates of Eating Problems in Chinese Male and Female Students Living in the United States," *International Journal of Eating Disorders,* Jan. 1999, 25 (1): 65–70.

[2] Goode, Erica. "Study of Fijian Girls Shows Effects of TV on Body Image, Eating Habits," *San Francisco Chronicle,* May 27, 1999."

What's Up with Boys and Eating Disorders?

Although we have written this book for young women, since this is where our experience and expertise is, it is also important to us to acknowledge young men. It's estimated that 10 percent of the eight million individuals with eating disorders in the United States are male, and that the rates of eating disorders among them are increasing. Recent figures on cosmetic surgery show that women still account for about 90 percent of all procedures, but the number of men having cosmetic surgery rose approximately 34 percent between 1996 and 1998, with liposuction being the most sought service.[1] In the gay community, there is a high risk factor of males' developing eating disorders because of the increased value placed on thinness. Approximately 20 percent of males with eating disorders are gay.[2]

Some argue that these statistics are too low, and that many young men with eating disorders are not diagnosed because 1) screening tests are biased toward females, 2) professionals see eating disorders as a primarily female disorder and therefore do not look for eating disorders in males, and 3) males are not as inclined to get help. Furthermore, when males do seek help, it is only available for women.[3] It is clear that more boys are struggling with food and weight than before. Eating disorders are no longer "just a girls' problem."

How Do Boys and Girls with Eating Disorders Differ?

In some ways boys and girls with eating disorders are very similar. They have similar feelings of body dissatisfaction, depression, and low self-esteem. However, there are some important differences in how boys and girls perceive their bodies and how the eating disorder affects their bodies. First of all, 75 percent to 80 percent of females with eating disorders want to lose weight, but only 40 percent of males with eating disorders want to *lose* weight, while the other 40 percent of males want to *gain* weight.[4] This makes sense because boys feel pressure not only to be thin, but also to be big and strong.

The *reasons* why males and females want to lose weight are also different. Males want to lose weight for specific reasons: 1) to improve athletic performance, 2) to avoid childhood teasing for being overweight, 3) to avoid medical illnesses due to weight problems, and 4) to improve homosexual relationships. Females, on the other hand, rarely have specific reasons for wanting to lose weight. They just want to lose weight to be thin, because weighing less means you are somehow good.[5] This is probably because females receive more *general* reinforcement for being thin and dieting, and males receive more specific pressure. Males with eating disorders are also more likely than females to be involved in a job or sport that is influenced by how much they weigh.[6]

Although both boys and girls with eating disorders don't like their bodies, they are dissatisfied with different parts of their bodies. Girls are primarily concerned with their waist down, while boys are primarily concerned with their waist up. Boys tend to be more concerned with their shape, and girls tend to be more concerned with their weight.[7] A study done in Hong Kong showed that boys wanted to be taller and stronger in their upper body; girls wanted to slim the stomach, thighs, waist, and hips, but not breasts.[8]

Other psychological characteristics of males and females with eating disorders tend to be similar. Depression, anxiety, obsessive/compulsive behavior, and drug abuse are all found in proportionate rates among males and females. However, post-traumatic stress from sexual abuse is much higher in females with eating disorders than in males with eating disorders.[9]

BOYS' BODIES

I feel like it's the same way as how girls have to look a certain way. There's definitely rules to how guys have to look a certain way too.

— Josh

Boys in our culture, as well as other cultures, are experiencing more pressure to have a certain body type: tall and buff. Look in any newspaper or magazine and you will see ads for males to strengthen their stomach muscles, develop "six-packs," buff up their chest and arms, look "cut" by defining their muscles, take steroids, get rid of baldness, and even get penile implants. Diets for men are surfacing more frequently on the covers of men's magazines.

Males are supposed to be tough and macho and have big muscles and stuff like that.

— Aaron

Ask any boy what the perfect male body is, and they will describe in their own words the same "V-shape." As Barbie continues to model the impossible ideal body type for girls, G.I. Joe and the Star Wars toys are becoming bigger and bulkier, creating an equally impossible ideal body type for males. Batman has the equivalent of a thirty-inch waist, fifty-seven-inch chest, and twenty-seven-inch biceps — not very realistic for the majority of young men.[10] Another cultural pressure boys face is immense peer pressure from other boys. "Fat boys" or "wimpy boys" are often teased and taunted by other boys, leading to chronic stress that can shape a boy's body image and self-image for life.

Hey, I have a girlfriend. That proves that my body is okay Right?

— P. W.

Like girls, boys seek approval of their bodies from the opposite sex. Their bodies are okay if they are desirable to the opposite sex. Boys talk about feeling pressure from girls wanting them to have big arms, strong stomachs, and no fat.

SPORTS AND STEROIDS

One guy, he's huge. He's a monster. He's so big, and he used to take steroids. Then he stopped taking them, and he was telling me about it. Steroids make you so much more aggressive. They give you a much shorter temper. Plus they give you heart problems and stuff. He was just saying, like, it's really not worth it.

— J. D.

Some guys pump up their bodies 'cause they are wieners inside. It's way more important to be strong in who you are than in what you look like.

— Dillon

One of the main reasons boys diet is to improve their athletic performance. Unlike most girls, many boys feel a pressure to excel in some kind of sports. Yet males who are involved in sports that require weight loss, such as runners, wrestlers, swimmers, and jockeys, are at a higher risk for eating disorders. A recent study showed that 78 percent of high school male athletes in Washington and Oregon used supplements, including creatine, ginseng, mahuange, and androstenedione.[11] And kids who use supplements are at a greater risk for using steroids. Unfortunately, there are serious health risks with steroids, including the risk of cardiovascular diseases, some forms of cancer, and shrinking of the testicles.

When I go to the weight room and see other people who are bigger than me, I want to try and get a body like theirs.

— Miguel

In one study done in 1993 among weight lifters who used steroids, 10 percent of them saw themselves as physically small and weak even though they were, in fact, large and muscular.[12] They call this syndrome "muscle dysmorphia." Body dysmorphic disorder used to be considered as mainly pertaining to women with anorexia who insisted they were fat even though they were emaciated. But imagining flaws in their appearance is becoming more common in males.

Boys and Feelings

Self-esteem is a mental game, kind of like skateboarding. In order to be a man, you've got to be able to hold your own and have a good head on your shoulders. You gotta always be up. Act like nothing can get you down.

— Izzy

Many boys in our culture do not talk about their feelings with their parents, other adults, or friends, because they are not encouraged to. Being "sensitive" or having feelings is perceived as being "weak." William Pollack, author of *Real Boys*, talks about how boys are caught between the old traditional view of males as being strong, tough, and self-sufficient, and the New Age view of men as sensitive, open, and communicative. Within this struggle, boys are searching for ways to express themselves that are acceptable and helpful.

Talking about your feelings actually makes you strong because it helps you deal with your emotions.

— Kyle

Instead of getting caught up in trying to be a physically strong guy, you can be emotionally strong by talking about your feelings. My role model is Chris Farley. He did not have a stereotypically perfect body, but he was awesome, the funniest guy in the world.

— Beau

Boys who are struggling with food and weight can find new and constructive ways to express their feelings regarding their insecurities, their body image, their fears, their needs, and their passions. It's important for them to be able to identify their needs, communicate them, and meet them. Boys often benefit from being in all-male support groups and from having male professionals as part of their treatment team. Although there tend to be fewer treatment programs for males with eating disorders than for females, there still are many individuals and programs that specialize in treating males with eating disorders.

Well, I'm six feet, five inches tall and wear size sixteen shoes. I have totally big things about me and that's something to get past. I feel comfortable to the point that I can joke around about it and make it a good thing.

— Josh

Learning to love and accept your natural body size is a struggle for anyone who has grown up in a culture that focuses on weight and appearance. Even though there are some differences between boys and girls with eating disorders, the bottom line is the same. Overeating, undereating, purging, and obsessing with food and weight are all ways to cope with emotional stresses like depression, low self-esteem, anxiety, and the inability to meet your own needs. Although males may have difficulty finding treatments that are not solely designed for females, research shows that males who complete treatment given by competent professionals have good outcomes. However, it's important for males to find a physician and mental-health therapist who will be sympathetic to the male perspective.

NOTES

[1] Hall, Stephen S., "The Troubled Life of Boys: The Bully in the Mirror," *New York Times Magazine,* August 22, 1999.

[2] Andersen, Arnold E. M.D., "Gender-Related Aspects of Eating Disorders: A Guide to Practice," *The Journal of Gender-Specific Medicine,* vol. 2 (1), 1999, 47–54.

[3] Ibid.

[4] Ibid.

[5] Ibid.

[6] Braun, Devral, Suzanne R. Sunday, Amy Huang, and Katherine A. Halmi, "More Males Seek Treatment for Eating Disorders," *International Journal of Eating Disorders,* vol. 25 (4), May 1999, pp. 415–24.

[7] Andersen, Arnold E. M.D., pp. 47–54.

[8] Lee, S., et al., "Body Dissatisfaction among Chinese Undergraduates and Its Implications for Eating Disorders in Hong Kong." *International Journal of Eating Disorders,* vol. 20 (1), July 1996, pp. 77–84.

[9] Andersen, Arnold E. M.D., pp. 47–54.

[10] Hall, Stephen S.

[11] Ibid.

[12] Ibid.

CHAPTER 9

Trusting Your Process

The bud
stands for all things,
even for those things that don't flower,
for everything flowers, from within, of self-blessing;
though sometimes it is necessary
to reteach a thing its loveliness,
to put a hand on the brow
of the flower
and retell it in words and in touch
it is lovely
until it flowers again from within, of self-blessing;

— Galway Kinnell, from "Saint Francis and the Sow"

As we heal from our struggles with food and weight, we are in the process of flowering. Like a tight rosebud that remains closed and protected from the world until it is ready to bloom, we too have remained curled up and protected within the walls of the obsession with food and weight. As we begin to relearn to love ourselves, to awaken ourselves, we allow ourselves to blossom from within. The blossoming occurs layer by layer, as each petal opens up, one by one, to greet the light.

It is not a linear process, and is therefore difficult to measure. You may be working on many different levels at once, yet feel like your behavior isn't changing at all. For example, maybe you are learning how to identify your feelings, and have learned to talk about them with someone, but still have the need to overeat or undereat. Maybe you are getting better at figuring out when you are hungry, but still have difficulty being conscious of when you are full. Maybe you have stopped bingeing or purging, but you still hate your body so much that the obsession with your weight is unbearable.

Because there are so many pieces to the puzzle, they don't all fall into place at once. We might pick up a piece, look at it, and know exactly where to put it. Then, we might pick up another piece, look at it, and have no clue where it goes. We then have to put it away and try to work with another piece. Often we are so focused on the outcome, the finished picture of the puzzle, that we forget we are taking very important steps necessary to create the picture itself. When this happens, we step into fear and judgment of ourselves, instead of acknowledging that with every piece we are building the picture. When we are so caught up in the daily struggle, we don't have perspective, and we can't see all of the pieces that fit into the puzzle. We only see what is in front of our face. This is why we have written this chapter, to offer you our perspective on the recovery process.

THE JOURNEY

I was in denial for a long time. I didn't even know I had an eating disorder. I just thought I was eating healthy. It wasn't until I was down to under a hundred pounds and I almost had to go to the hospital to be fed intravenously that I really realized I was in trouble. Then it took me a long time to trust that I was on the right path. It was so painful to go through the stuff I was going through. I had an eating disorder for some pretty deep reasons and I needed to really see if those reasons were worth it anymore. I was in a group and I also had a therapist that I could talk to and eventually I could open up and share what was going on for me. It was better when I saw that they were going through the same stuff and that I wasn't alone. But as I was going through it, I learned a lot about me. And I found out that I could go through life without this problem.

— Lindsey

During the recovery process, it is easy to feel bogged down, overwhelmed, and hopeless. This recovery is like going on a vision quest with a winding path that turns so often that it is hard to see ahead of you and impossible to see behind. There is one challenging obstacle after another. Sometimes it feels like you are getting somewhere, and sometimes it feels like you are going around in circles. It's times like these that you feel like you just have to have blind faith. You do! However, we have found that it is also helpful to get an idea of what other people's recovery process looks like so that you can have a visual map to look at when you feel like you are lost.

We have created a map of this journey. In our work we found that there seems to be a pattern to the different stages that people go through. The stages start with denial of the problem and end with complete freedom from the problem. This is not to say that everyone's process is the same. Quite the contrary! Everyone's process is unique. But there are similarities and these are what we will talk about in this chapter. Remember, everyone's "path" is different. There is no "right way." This map is simply a guideline.

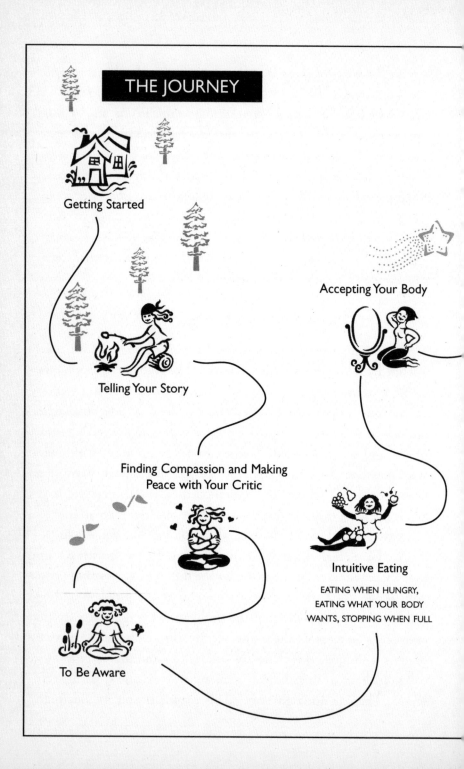

THE JOURNEY

Getting Started

Telling Your Story

Accepting Your Body

Finding Compassion and Making
Peace with Your Critic

Intuitive Eating

EATING WHEN HUNGRY,
EATING WHAT YOUR BODY
WANTS, STOPPING WHEN FULL

To Be Aware

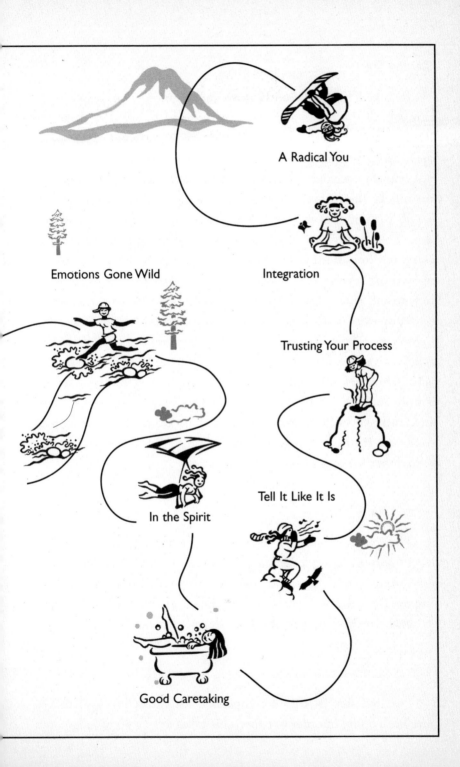

A Radical You

Integration

Emotions Gone Wild

Trusting Your Process

In the Spirit

Tell It Like It Is

Good Caretaking

Getting Started

It takes time, patience, love, acceptance, and *work* to go through all the twists and turns of the road to recovery. Like the flower bud that slowly opens as it matures, our deepest selves slowly open as we get more and more insight to our behavior. This does not happen overnight. It takes as long as it takes and no one can rush it. In the recovery from eating disorders, there are many layers of learning that will unfold in their own time and in their own way. We call this part of the journey "trusting your process." It is extremely important to trust yourself as you go through the process of learning how to feed yourself, to take care of yourself, to listen to yourself, and to love yourself unconditionally — *no matter what.*

Your work is to find your path through the challenges along the journey. This map is only to tell you where some of the peaks, valleys, rivers, volcanoes, and rocks might be. How *you* go on the path is how *you* are supposed to go. There is no wrong way. There is only your way. And when you listen to your own inner wisdom and truth, you will know what that way is. Do not use our map as your own truth, but only as a guideline to find your own truth. Remember: *trust your process.*

Telling Your Story

The journey begins by reflection — by telling your own story. It's important to explore how your eating disorder has helped you get through your life so far. As you tell your own story, you will empower yourself with new understanding about your own unique struggle. In this way you can take steps to change.

Finding Compassion and Making Peace with Your Critic

The first step is to find compassion for yourself and what you have been doing in order to cope. This takes letting go of judgment, for yourself and your eating disorder. It means understanding how your eating disorder has tried to take care of you. As much as you can, let go of harsh, critical self-judgments that you have learned from others and taken on as your own. Work on developing the non-judgmental observer that can help you to explore yourself as kindly as possible. In other words, give yourself a break.

To Be Aware

This is the time that you will begin to come out of denial. It is impossible to do this if you don't get off your own case. It's way too painful. What we're asking you to do is look straight into the face of your eating disorder. YIPES! We're telling you to really look at and become aware of how you are overeating, undereating, bingeing, purging, compulsively dieting, or exercising. We're also asking you to see how much hatred you have for your own body, and to bring awareness to why you do the things you do or think the things you think.

Self-Hatred

As you come out of denial, the first thing to pop up is often hatred for the years that you spent having an eating disorder, and hatred for the way you have treated yourself because you have an eating disorder. You might be surprised, as you become conscious of your thoughts and feelings, at how much hatred you feel for your body and yourself. This is very painful, but it is also completely natural to have these emotions at this stage. If you will allow yourself to go through these very uncomfortable feelings, you will see that your self-hatred has been taught to you.

Anger

Anger usually comes up early in the recovery process — anger at the culture you live in, anger at yourself for not being able to "control" your behavior, or anger at family members and friends. It may be scary to feel this, but anger is a very powerful and necessary emotion. You can learn to be angry without being destructive to yourself or anyone else. You can use this stage for transformation by redirecting your anger and expressing it in constructive ways. This transformation is the path to freedom.

Intuitive Eating

This is the stage where you stop dieting and start listening to your own internal signals of hunger, desire, and fullness. You begin to let *all* food be legal. There is no "good" food, no "bad" food, no "fattening" food, no "junk" food, no "better" food, no "legal" food. There is only "food." When you feel hungry, the only question to ask yourself is "What does my body want to eat right now?" And then, as much as possible, let yourself have it. The only way to do this is to let go of control. This must be done. If you try to control what you eat, you are back on a diet. What you are trying to do is let your body tell you what you want to eat, and trust in your body's wisdom to answer your own call of hunger. You are trying to learn how you are as a "natural eater." At this point some girls gain weight. Don't freak out! Some girls lose weight and some girls stay the same. IT'S NOT ABOUT FAT! IT'S NOT ABOUT WEIGHT! The most important thing to remember right now is that you don't have any idea what your body is supposed to weigh. Let go of all scales. Listen to your hunger, listen to your body, listen to your inner self. Every *body* is different. Stay with yourself and your process in order to go all the way though the next stage.

Rebellion

During this stage, the rebel comes to town. This is the time when many girls start to rebel against all the years of deprivation:

deprivation of food, deprivation of happiness with your body and yourself. It is not unusual to overeat at this stage. You might just be trying to make up for all that you have been denied. Or you might go through a stage of not wanting to be a "good," "pretty," or "sweet" girl. Believe it or not, this is a good thing. When you realize that you don't have to rebel with food and weight, but instead, rebel against the culture that has been trying to put you in a tiny box, then you will be through one of the hardest parts of the process. It's also natural that in young adulthood you want to rebel. You are supposed to. It's your job. You are finding out who you really are and what you really want.

Practicing Eating

When you are letting yourself eat when you are hungry, eat what your body wants, and stop when you are full, you are taking care of yourself in the most awesome way there is. If a lot of the time you still overeat, undereat, or obsess about how you look, be patient and keep on keeping on. This stage of the process takes as long as it takes. You cannot rush this part. Actually, you can't rush any part of this process, but especially not this part. Sometimes you are able to eat when you're hungry, but you don't know what it is that you want to eat. Sometimes you can't stop eating when you know you are full, but you know exactly what you want to eat. Sometimes everything falls in line perfectly, and sometimes nothing seems to be getting better. It is getting better. You are learning. You are experimenting. You are going up and down and around and around the mountain. You are practicing. Like any other skill (even one you were born with), it takes a lot of patience and practice before you can do it without even thinking about it. Someday this will happen. Stay committed to being a nonjudgmental observer and just notice and practice.

Fear and Panic

As you start to completely let go of all control and eat foods you used to think were bad, in amounts that you used to think were too much, and not worry about what other people tell you to do, it's easy to flip out. It's not unusual to think that you are going to gain a million pounds or that you're going to blow up like a balloon. Or you may experience pure terror at who you are going to be if you're not "the girl with the eating disorder." You might get scared that you are going to be fat, unhappy, gross, and disgusting if you don't at least *try* to control yourself or your weight. This is normal and it's scary. And it's a necessary part of the process. What we always say at this point to the girls in our groups is "Well, how did it work before?" They answer, "Usually not very well." Controlling food and weight rarely works. *Diets don't work!* So each time the fear and panic hits, remind yourself that 1) you are not on a diet, 2) it's not about fat or food, and 3) there is always another chance to take care of yourself by eating when you're hungry, eating what you want, and stopping when you're full. Breathe, come back to yourself, love yourself, and move on to the next challenge of the journey.

Accepting Your Body

This challenge of the journey is to learn to accept your natural body type. This means creating a completely different relationship with your body. It might mean letting go of what you think your body *should* look like. It means to trust your body, treat it with respect, and stop beating it up!

Emotions Gone Wild

Welcome to the wild river of feelings. At this part of the journey you begin to notice the undercurrent of feelings. As you become more aware, you start to figure out what feelings are flow-ing and where. Some may just trickle by you, while others may go crashing through you. But with practice you learn to navigate your way through them. Whenever you find yourself eating when you're not physically hungry, or not eating when you are physically hungry, or obsessing, remember to look at what is happening on a "feeling" level. Something is going on. What is it? Ask yourself, "What am I feeling?" or "What do I really need?" or "How can I give this to myself?" And then listen for the answer.

In the Spirit

This part of the process is one that you will practice all of your entire life as you grow and shift and change. This is where you can start to discover who you are as a spiritual being. By healing your own spiritual wounds, you will free the creative and powerful force of your soul. This will lead you to your spiritual calling, buried underneath the layers of your eating disorder. Keep working on expanding your faith in your higher self, and trust that it will carry you through the rough and tough parts of the journey yet to come.

Good Caretaking

Feeling your feelings, eating *when* you want to, *what* you want to, and *how much* you want to are all great examples of taking care of yourself. Each time you match your needs and wants with the appropriate response, you feed your soul. When you feed your soul, you prove to yourself that *you can* and *you will* always take care of yourself. This is how you become your own best friend. This is how you build up trust in yourself and your ability to handle anything that happens to you in your life. When you know you will take care of yourself, *no matter what,* you can do anything. Each time you pay attention to yourself, and listen to the voice within, you are taking care of yourself.

As you go within and understand the things you need, want, and desire, and then without judgment or blame, give them to yourself, you expand your trust and love for yourself. This is when you start to fall in love with yourself. This is when you know that you are always on your own side. You are learning to accept your body, *exactly as it is,* and learning to let go of any need to change it. Keep learning to love, support, and trust yourself. That is what best friends do. Be your own best friend.

Tell It Like It Is

"Telling it like it is" means speaking and living your truth. It is standing on top of the mountain and letting the world know who you are. You can learn to say no, set limits, express your truth, and take a stand.

Trusting Your Process

As you enter this stage of the journey, it starts to heat up. As you put your food and your weight in perspective, all the feelings that you once ate over, starved over, or threw up over start bubbling up and out like lava in a volcano. These are the feelings that have been buried beneath your eating disorder.

This place, on top of the erupting volcano, is where you have all of your feelings and you still have the eating disorder behavior. You have the feelings that you hate and the behavior that you hate. You will experience frustration, hopelessness, and feelings of being overwhelmed. Though it does not feel like it, this is a very powerful place in your recovery.

Anger, sadness, loneliness, grief, and inner-child issues are some of the feelings that begin to surface. Old childhood wounds, caused by neglect, abandonment, rejection, or physical or sexual abuse may come up for you and be confusing. Things you thought didn't really bother you before might bother you now. Old hurts and disappointments that you thought you had let go of might come back. This is part of the process. No matter how hurt you might be, or how scared you are to feel these old wounds, don't give up.

These feelings have always been there — you just weren't aware of them. It is an illusion to believe you didn't feel them before. They were buried where you thought they couldn't hurt you. And now you can see that they did. Remember that you are learning how to be strong enough to see them, feel them, and deal with them. You have dealt with them before, the only way you could. Now you are learning a different way. You are getting tools to be able to handle your life and the feelings of your life. Have faith.

This might be the time when you need a trusted friend, therapist, or support group to help you deal with these very tough feelings. Let yourself have whatever you need. Do not deny yourself in any way. Get the support you need, want, and deserve to really go within and let out the pain you have held within. Keep breathing and keep loving yourself, unconditionally.

The Volcano Erupts

I swear to God there's a map of the recovery process and there's a point on the top where it's like you have all this wisdom. You know dieting is bad, compulsive eating is not what you want to do, and not listening to your body is not a good thing, but you don't have full acceptance yet. Right? So it's like, where do you go? But the thing is to keep trying and then it changes and you pretty much have to keep accepting and move. And then you go on over the top and it's like you're leaping off a cliff. And it's great.

— Maggie

We couldn't have said it better. What Maggie is describing is the most difficult part of recovery. It's the part where you have all the insight in the world, but you still have the behavior that makes you so unhappy. To make matters worse, eating, starving, or obsessing doesn't really work anymore. You still feel lousy. If you are an overeater, you know diets don't work. If you are an under-eater, you know that controlling and starving don't work. You can hardly bear the feelings you are having. You feel like you're going crazy. You can't stand yourself, your body, or this frigging process.

This is the most difficult part of the whole process.

There is no doubt about it. It sucks. It's terrible. It's bad. Frustration and hopelessness are the two most common feelings at this time. You have been working hard to stop these behaviors, but you still feel the feelings that you used to go to such great lengths not to feel! Your thoughts are full of how fat and ugly you are. You can't wait to starve or stuff. Even though you know it won't work, you still are doing it. You feel frustrated, over-whelmed, and hopeless.

You are still learning to have the faith and trust you need to go through this part of the process. As painful as it is, when you get to the other side, you will see how necessary and powerful it is. This part of the process will teach you about yourself as nothing else can. No book, no teacher, no parent, no school, no nothing will show you what you will be shown by watching yourself go through this.

You will learn love and faith. You will learn just how strong you are. You will be at peace with yourself. You will learn who you really are and what you really want to do. You will eventually eat like a normal person. You will weigh what you are supposed to weigh, according to what is best for your own unique body. You will know and speak your truth. You will truly experience joy, laughter, happiness, peace, sadness, grief, and most of all, *life*. This is the top of the volcano. Even if you go back and forth over the top and back down again, don't despair. Just keep listening to your body, keep working on accepting your body, keep feeling your feelings, keep trusting, and keep loving yourself all the way through this. You are steadily recovering. You are going for the cure. You are the greatest.

Integration

At this stage of the journey you will notice that all of the work you have been doing is starting to stick — maybe not all of the time, but some of the time. As you continue to feel your feelings, it will become more comfortable to express them and take care of yourself emotionally. On a day-to-day basis, as feelings arise, you will find you have other tools to deal with them. You may still be bingeing, starving, or obsessing, but the urgency and frequency is slowly declining as you learn to process the emotional issues.

Letting Go of Old Behaviors

At this point in the process you will find that you are starting to experience small miracles in relationship to your food. If your pattern is undereating, you will find yourself becoming more comfortable eating when you are hungry. You will actually be able to intervene when you find yourself not eating and, instead, choose to feed yourself based on your hunger. If your history is bulimia, you will experience letting yourself sit with the fullness, not having to purge each time you eat. You will have more tools to process the fears of becoming fat or anxious if you don't purge. If you overeat, you will be able to stop yourself, ask yourself if you are hungry, and if not, give yourself what you really need. These mini-miracles will become more consistent every day until you are able, more often than not, to let go of the overeating and undereating.

Mourning the Loss of the Food

As you begin to let go of the struggle with food, it becomes what it was always meant to be, just something to eat when you are hungry. It loses all of its old meaning, charge, and drama. It no longer works like it used to. It fades into the background, sometimes leaving behind a feeling of emptiness. Feeling sad that your relationship with food has changed is normal. Feeling scared because of the emptiness, or even bittersweet because of how the food took care of you for so long, is also normal. Your feelings will be unique to you, but if you find yourself having feelings of loss or sadness, remember that for many women this is part of the process.

Reduction in Obsessive Thinking about Food and Weight

As you become more aware of the link between your feelings and your thoughts about food and weight, you will develop more tools to bring your awareness back to what you really need. With time, the obsessive thinking begins to slow down. You will find that it is easier to concentrate in school or in conversation with other people. You can be more present in your life because you won't always be thinking about what you should and shouldn't eat or look like. This doesn't mean that it will completely disappear — there may still be many times when something triggers a fat thought or a food thought. Now, however, when this happens, you will have the tools to see it, stop it, and find out what you really need.

A Transformed Relationship to Food and Your Body

Can you imagine walking into a room full of food and feeling completely at ease? Can you imagine not having to worry about what you weigh? Can you imagine not having to plan what you are going to eat that day, or not feeling guilty or wrong for eating a certain food? Your relationship with food has completely changed. No longer does food hold an emotional charge. Eating becomes a normal, natural pleasure. It can feel a bit strange at first, and also a bit alienating when everyone else around you is still afraid or critical of food. But you'll also feel free to have a choice about what you want to eat and when you want to eat it.

Your relationship with your body also changes. You no longer hate it and call it horrible names. You begin to have respect for what is uniquely yours. You might find it uncomfortable when someone makes a comment about your body — or even someone else's. You might be super aware of how often other women make negative comments about their own bodies. Whereas the comments used to seem normal, now that you no longer hate your body, they may seem a little silly to you. You might find yourself feeling more comfortable going places and doing things without having to worry about how you look. As your relationship to your body continues to change, you will find ways to keep honoring and respecting it.

Recognizing a Signal for Help

When you find yourself wanting to eat when you are not hungry, or obsessing about food and weight, or restricting your eating when you are hungry, you are able to be conscious of it and to immediately see your behavior. You now have the tools to say, "Isn't this interesting, I'm having a fat thought!" You can look within, find out what feelings are lying underneath the behavior, process these feelings, and take care of yourself.

Continued Emotional Processing

When you recover from an eating disorder, it doesn't mean you will not have any more problems for the rest of your life. It means you have learned to listen to your physical, emotional, and spiritual needs, and now you can take care of yourself. Life will still have its ups and downs, and its joys and sorrows. However, now you are able to be with yourself through these challenges in a loving and nurturing way. You don't have to turn to overeating, undereating, or obsessing. You can now walk with yourself through whatever challenges come up. You also know how to ask for help and get support if you feel like you need it. For the rest of your life, you will have these tools to process whatever emotions arise.

Acceptance, Love, and Trust in Yourself

As you learn to accept and trust your body and your own process in regard to your eating disorder, you will also find this happening in other areas of your life. You may find yourself trusting yourself more in relationships, jobs, school, sports, or any other area in your life that you find challenging. You may find that you are more accepting of your imperfections and can give yourself more room to experiment and learn. You may also find that you are more in touch with how you feel about certain issues and what your opinions are.

Reaching Your Natural Weight

Your natural weight occurs when you eat when you're hungry, eat what your body is hungry for, and stop when you are full. Your body will find the size and shape that is genetically natural for you. Whether you gain weight, lose weight, or maintain weight will depend upon genetics and your type of eating disorder. How long it takes to reach your natural weight is different for everyone. We have put it at the end of the journey because it often takes a while for weight to stabilize.

Reaching your natural weight may bring new challenges. It may be difficult to accept that you are a different weight than what you thought you should be. Or you may find yourself forced to deal with people's comments about your weight loss or gain. You may notice that your old weight protected you from something that you now need to face — sexuality, relationships, or responsibility. However, once again, you have the tools to take care of yourself around these challenges and find support if you need it.

A Radical You

As you begin to heal from the struggle with food and weight, you will feel blessed with a sense of freedom:

- freedom from restricting your food
- freedom from bingeing
- freedom from constantly worrying about what you should or shouldn't eat
- freedom from hating your body and always worrying about being too fat
- freedom from feeling insecure about yourself
- freedom to make your own choices about your food, your body, your desires, and your life
- freedom to follow your passion

You will have found your own unique, divine, and radical self!

THE SPIRAL

Imagine a great big, three-dimensional spiral, starting from the ground and climbing up into the sky. The process of healing is much more like this spiral than a straight line. We've found it helpful to remember this spiral when it feels like we've gotten nowhere, or like we've somehow "blown it" and are back at square one.

We often think of the healing process as a game of Monopoly, where if we do some behavior we are trying to stop (throwing up, bingeing, or eating a forbidden food), we have to "go to jail, directly to jail, do not pass Go, do not collect $200." But remember that each time we do something that we are trying to stop, it is an opportunity to learn more about ourselves. If we are willing to stay compassionate, nonjudgmental, and inquisitive, we can take this experience and use it as a building block in our healing. Instead of "going directly to jail," we can go to another level of understanding and problem solving.

This is why we believe the healing process is more like a spiral than a straight line. You may bump up against the same behavior over and over again, but if you can learn from each occurrence, you move yourself up the spiral each time. Eventually the behavior is no longer necessary.

We've also known many people who have gone for a long time without struggling with food and weight, who start old behaviors again when, all of a sudden, something happens in their lives. They get scared and think, "Oh my God, I've lost all my recovery and now I'm back at the beginning!" But this really isn't true. They might be on the same side of the spiral, in the place where they are doing the old behaviors again, but they have all of these other layers of recovery underneath them. They know how to work themselves out of it. They already know how to observe themselves without judgment and become conscious of what they are doing. They know how to bring their awareness back to eating when hungry, stopping when full, and eating what feels right for their bodies. They can take care of themselves emotionally and spiritually, and ask for help. So they will be able to work themselves back around the circle of the spiral more quickly and easily than before.

If you find yourself thinking you have "blown it" and are hopelessly back at the beginning, remember the image of the spiral and all of the circles of growth that you have as a foundation beneath you.

TRY THIS: Trusting Your Process

1. Draw your own map of your process of recovery. It can look like ours or it can be completely different.
2. On a daily basis for a week, write down somewhere on your map something about where you are in your recovery process. Focus on giving yourself credit for something you did each day, even if it's just "I survived today!"
3. Whenever you feel like you have failed or aren't making any progress, draw the spiral and remind yourself of all of the layers of growing you have done since the beginning of this process. Mark on the circles of the spirals what they represent in terms of your growth up to today, so you can see how much of a foundation you have underneath you already. Use these spirals to help you focus on how you can support yourself now.

In this recovery, each individual has her own path on the journey. There may be many others you greet along the way who can help you climb up a boulder or cross a river, but no one can walk your path for you. Your path is as unique as your own body and soul. When you can start to trust yourself, you will realize that you are not bad or wrong because of where you are on the journey. You are just *you*, a very precious and unique being who is learning to navigate life.

A Radical You

Whether or not you are aware of it yet, your struggle with food and weight is providing you with an opportunity to find and fall in love with yourself. It is opening up a pathway to become radical. The word radical stems from the word *radicalis* meaning having roots. To be radical means to reach all the way through to the center, to the ultimate source. This is what recovering from an eating disorder requires you to do. You must go beneath the obsession with food and weight, and find your way to your soul.

In this way, an eating disorder can become a precious gift. Although we curse it, hate it, and feel like it is killing us, it is actually a very sacred part of us. Even though the behaviors are hurting us, they are born of the desire to take care of ourselves by coping however we can. As we open our hearts to our struggle and let it teach us, we receive many gifts. We learn to have compassion for ourselves and others. We learn to respond to ourselves with curiosity and love instead of harsh judgment. We begin to listen to the wisdom of our bodies, meet our hungers, and appreciate the miracle of our own unique body types. We learn to understand what we need emotionally and take steps to nurture ourselves. We begin to hear our own voices, experience our spiritual selves, and respond to the passion and creativity within us. We express ourselves, learning to live in a way that honors our own unique truth. We find out how to trust the unfolding of our selves as we transform from caterpillar to butterfly. And most simply, we learn to love ourselves.

We know that this might seem like a miracle to you. It was to us. As we were struggling with our food and weight, bingeing and purging, stuffing and starving, and all the time hating ourselves, recovery seemed impossible. It was hopeless. It seemed like no matter what we tried, nothing worked. But as we continued to search, continued to seek help, little by little we began to listen. It was not easy, and it was not quick. But it was worth it.

We want you to know that miracles are possible. You *can* recover from your struggle with food and weight and live a happy and fulfilling life. We hope that this book supports you in that process, and most of all, leads you back to your precious, radical self.

For Parents

If you are not sure whether your child has an eating disorder or needs professional help, seek professional advice. For referrals, call EDAP at (800) 931-2237.

If you are reading this, chances are you are lucky enough to be involved in your child's eating disorder. Our parents weren't. We weren't able to discuss it with our families until long after we had been through the recovery process as adults. We missed the opportunity to receive the support and the growth that can happen in families when an individual struggles with food and weight. We tell you this because we want you to know that even though it is a painful, frightening process to witness a child with an eating disorder, it is also an opportunity to grow and learn about yourself, your child, and your family.

We see eating disorders as a cry from the soul, a cry to search beneath the obsession with food and weight to find one's true self. As your child struggles with learning to feed her body and soul, you too will be forced to struggle — maybe in similar ways, maybe in different ways. The way you choose to deal with her eating disorder will have an impact on her. You may not be able to control her behavior, you may not be able to stop her from hurting her body, but you can let her know, moment by moment, that you love and respect her.

When we become parents, we are not given many tools. We face many challenges that we have not been prepared to deal with, in our relationships with our partners, our families, our culture, and within ourselves. There were no mandatory classes in high school or college on basic parenting. So when we feel confused, ineffective, or responsible regarding our children, we are not bad parents. It is understandable that there will be times in our parenting when we need help. Having a child who struggles with food and weight is one of those times.

We have written this section to support you in getting help for yourself and your child. Here are ten things you can do as a parent to support your child with an eating disorder:

1. Have compassion for yourself, your child, and your family.
2. Educate yourself.
3. Get support for yourself and your child.
4. Model self-love and acceptance.
5. Stop unnecessary dieting.
6. Support your child's natural physiological cues of hunger and fullness.
7. Give your child the responsibility to select his/her own food.
8. Teach self-esteem from within.
9. Help your child identify, express, and resolve feelings.
10. Be an activist in your community.

Have Compassion for Yourself, Your Child, and Your Family

I don't know what it would be like for me to have kids. I think I would be a bad mother because when I try and have love and compassion and nurturing and understanding for myself, I can't do it because that's not what I've gotten from my mother.... It's messing up my life with my self, my mother, and my friends, my

*everything. So for parents to be compassionate and to be caring
and supportive is just so important.*

— Nat

Compassion is essential for any parent who has a child with an
eating disorder. It is a very difficult process to go through. You
may find yourself feeling guilty, angry, victimized, stupid, embarrassed, scared, responsible, or any number of feelings. But it is
important to meet yourself every step of the way with compassion.
You are doing your best as a parent, and your child is doing her
best as a child. You, your child, and your family deserve to be supported, loved, and held with compassion throughout this healing
process. If you have trouble being compassionate, find a therapist,
friend, or partner who can give you compassion. Your child needs
you to find compassion for yourself so that you can offer it to her.

EDUCATE YOURSELF

By age nine, 31 percent of female children reported
fear of becoming fat. By age ten, 81 percent reported a
fear of becoming fat. Among nine to ten-year-old girls,
51 percent reported feeling better about themselves if
they were on a diet.[1] Thirty-five percent of "normal
dieters" progress to pathological dieting. Of those, 20 to
25 percent progress to partial or full-syndrome eating disorders.[2]

The first step in helping a child with an eating disorder is
educating yourself. There is a lot of information available about
eating disorders. There are books, articles, Web sites, and

national organizations (see Resources). Learn about the causes of eating disorders. Eating disorders are very complex and different for everyone, so explore what might be most applicable to your child. Explore your own issues regarding food and weight, as well. Look at what you learned growing up, and try to understand how this has affected your relationship with food and weight. Understand your role as a parent in the treatment of eating disorders. How can you support your child, and yourself, in a productive way? Understanding eating disorders will allow you to have both compassion and the tools you need to support your child.

GET SUPPORT FOR YOURSELF AND YOUR CHILD

If your child has an eating disorder, it is important to get her to a physician who works with eating disorders to make sure she is not at risk physically. It may also be important to meet with a nutritionist, depending upon your child's history. Find a qualified therapist who can work with the psychological issues. Find out about what other resources are available for you and your child, such as support groups.

As a parent of a child with an eating disorder, don't neglect yourself. It is extremely important to get support for yourself. It can be a frightening, frustrating process, and you need to have a place to express your feelings and get support from others who can help or understand. Many therapists specialize in working with parents of children with eating disorders, and there are also support groups for these parents.

One of the most effective ways to support your child is to work on your own issues. Not only does this model for your child the process of taking responsibility for your own recovery and working through problems, it also helps you cope with your own internal problems so that you can be more present with your child.

MODEL SELF-LOVE AND ACCEPTANCE

I want to tell parents to be a role model. You can't expect to have a kid that has a really healthy body image and eating behavior if you're sitting there dieting, and doing that little exercise schedule thing, going to the gym every day, and buying all nonfat organic food. It's just not going to happen. You pass on your values, you pass on your looks, you pass on a lot of things to your kids, and you're not going to escape passing on your attitudes towards body image. That's the most important thing.

— Vanessa

Being a role model is one of the most powerful ways of teaching our children. As Vanessa suggests, we pass on so much, just by who we are and what we do day to day. Unfortunately, the majority of women in our culture today are unhappy with their bodies and diet frequently. This is modeled very clearly to our youth. If you find you are struggling with your own weight or body image, get help for yourself. Find a support group, start therapy, or read our book for adults, *It's Not about Food*.

I see my mom pinch her thighs and say, "Oh, you are so ugly!" and then I look in the mirror and see the same thing. How can I think that my thighs are anything but ugly too?

— Tiffany

Our children see us looking in the mirror from the time they are tiny. They learn from us, they emulate us, and they believe us. If we have issues with our own bodies that we haven't worked out, they can see that, and they will take it on as their own issue, especially if they have a similar body type genetically.

I think the one thing parents can do that I still wish my parents would've done is to not bash themselves and other people. I can remember so many times hearing my mom sit there and say, "Oh, that person doesn't look right in that." And don't compare your children to each other. I used to get compared to my sister all the time. My sister is older than me and skinnier than me, and my dad would joke to her: "You better be nice or your sister might sit on you, she's bigger than you now." If parents would realize that even if they're not talking about their child, their child is still hearing it, and it's going to affect them.

— Jennifer

Even if you never say anything negative directly to your child about her body, but hold judgments about certain body types, your child will feel this. Avoid making critical comments about your own and other's weight or body parts, and work on your own issues of body hatred and sizism (prejudice against large body types), so that you can model self-love, self-acceptance, and self-respect. If you provide your child with enough of that at home, it will help her to combat the constant negative messages coming at her on a daily basis in our culture.

Teach your child critical thinking about societal messages regarding sizism and the obsession with thinness. Sizism is one of the last prejudices that is still somewhat acceptable. It's essential for young people to learn to question what they are told by advertisements, television, and movies.

STOP UNNECESSARY DIETING

I started off just wanting to "eat healthy" and then it became real extreme and I just wanted to see how much weight I could lose. As I got thinner and thinner, I thought it was a good thing. People thought I was more attractive. But then, later on people started going, "Euuuu, you're sooo skinny." So, I started to hide it. Then people saw what was going on but no one knew what to do. I pulled away from everyone because I didn't want to deal with their worries or questions. For me, I didn't think what I was doing was so wrong because I got so much attention for how thin I was. But finally my mom took me to a counselor and even though I was so mad at first, later on it finally made me see what was happening to me.

— Kristin

Dieting is a precursor to eating disorders. Diets rarely work, and dieting can be dangerous! Ninety-five percent of all dieters regain their lost weight within one to five years. Be aware that so-called "good" or "healthy" eating can be another form of dieting. Dieting in puberty can retard normal healthy female development and identity formation. Dieting can have serious negative health consequences, including loss of muscle strength and endurance, decreased oxygen utilization, loss of muscle glycogen and blood flow to the kidneys, reduced blood volume and heart function, and electrolyte imbalance.

Dieting can encourage the diet/binge cycle and lead to eating disorders. Individuals who diet are eight times more likely to develop eating disorders. Dieting can also lead to psychologically harmful effects, like irritability, impaired judgment and critical thinking, low self-esteem, obsessiveness, feelings of worthlessness, and mood swings — including depression so severe it can lead to suicide. Dieting also disregards the messages the body gives about hunger and fullness, and does not address the cultural and psychological issues underlying the struggles with food and weight.

When I was younger I was always trying to be thin. And so I stopped eating and was going hungry all the time. I got really depressed and couldn't sleep. I was in a lot of pain — all to be thin.

— Caitlin

There are many girls that go to bed hungry every night. Not because they are poverty stricken, not because they are homeless, not because they live in a depressed area, but because they are trying to be thin and they are on a diet. As we've said above, dieting in the adolescent years can have a devastating, lasting effect on physical and mental health. As young bodies are growing and changing, teens often start to put on fat in the areas that make them female: the hips, thighs, and breasts. Because the culture we live in tells us that "fat is bad," the teens counteract that by struggling to stay thin and "fat free." Remember that young bodies naturally shift and change. What they look like starting out may not be what they look like at the end of adolescence.

The dieting industry is a multimillion-dollar industry. Its main goal is to keep people unhappy about how they look. That is how the diet industry makes its money.

Teaching your child the hazards of dieting, and supporting her as she learns to listen to her hunger and fullness, will help her become a natural eater. Another way you can do this is by modeling intuitive eating for her. If you're not sure how to do this, and many women aren't, get help and learn how.

SUPPORT YOUR CHILD'S NATURAL PHYSIOLOGICAL CUES OF HUNGER AND FULLNESS

Sometimes I eat a lot and sometimes I don't eat anything. It just goes in stages or something. But everyone has to make comments all the time. Then I think maybe they know when I'm hungry more than I do. But how can that be right?

— Ami

Children are born with natural cues that tell them when to eat, what to eat, and when to stop. Rigid rules about eating can undermine these cues and invalidate the child's physiological needs for food. Even reminders like "Don't eat that, you'll spoil your appetite," or "Clean your plate for all of the starving children in India," can have that effect, with repetition. A child with an eating disorder has lost touch with her natural cues. Overeaters have learned to eat when they are not hungry, while undereaters have learned just the opposite, not to eat when they are hungry. It's important for people with eating disorders to get back in touch with their natural cues, hunger, fullness, and desire. When they can start to listen to their physiological cues, they begin to see that when they override those cues, there is usually a psychological process taking over.

If we, as parents, have been dieters and don't have faith in our own ability to choose what we need and want, then it's hard to teach our children how to identify their own needs and wants. The work for us is to learn to trust our internal wisdom, to become our own "diet experts" by listening to our physical bodies' messages when they tell us we are hungry, what kind of food would be the most satisfying to us, and when we are full. We all have this ability. We may not know it yet, but we do.

GIVE YOUR CHILD THE RESPONSIBILITY TO SELECT HIS/HER OWN FOOD

The other day I was really hungry and I wanted to eat a candy bar and everyone in my family said to me, "Are you sure you want to eat that?" Yeah, I'm sure. I picked it, didn't I?

— Jennifer

If you educate children about nutrition, teach them to listen to how their bodies respond to different types of food, and allow them to choose their own foods, they will learn to trust their own decision making about what to eat. If your child has a serious eating disorder, it is imperative that she sees a doctor and nutritionist.

These professionals can help stabilize your child physically. But as a parent, trying to control what your child eats can set up a power struggle that you will never win. When you can give up unnecessary control and struggles over food, children often become more willing to listen to information geared to help them make good decisions for themselves.

We are so used to worrying about what our children are eating that we forget they have the ability to choose what they want to eat. This ability must be nurtured and cared for. When they are allowed to recover their innate ability to be natural eaters, they will never completely lose it. Young children already know how to listen to their bodies' cues, hunger, desire, and satisfaction. We just need to be there to remind them. One of our jobs as parents is to provide an abundance of different and nutritious foods, but not to make any one food or group of foods "wrong."

One of the things we teach in our groups at Beyond Hunger is to get away from the notion that there is "bad" food or "good" food. There is only food. Some foods for some people work better than others. That is why it is important to allow your child to listen to what her body says about certain foods. This is a much more constructive process than the constant fighting that sometimes goes on around meal times. It is extremely hard to let go of the control that we in this culture have been taught to have around food and weight. But we believe it is much better to teach our children how to feed themselves in a way that honors them for who they are and how their own bodies need to be. The greatest gift we can give ourselves and our children is the gift of self-trust and self-reliance.

TEACH SELF-ESTEEM FROM WITHIN

In the movies they always show how the thin, pretty girls get everything they want. That's why all the little girls want to look

*like the little mermaid, with the big breasts and the tiny waist.
Also, they show the big girls are the "evil" ones. The mean and
ugly stepsisters are always fat. Even if a girl is chubby, she only
gets the guy if she gets it together and loses weight by the end of
the movie. And even if she doesn't lose weight and the guy loves
her anyway, it's like this sympathy thing like, "Oh, isn't it nice
that he's staying with the fat girl." It's so sick!*

— Kaitlin

It is so sick and our girls know it. Good is associated with one
body type and bad is associated with another.

Children face severe cultural pressures to conform to an unrealistic body type. The culture we live in teaches girls that they can
make money using their bodies through advertising, marriage,
entertainment, prostitution, and pornography. The more the
body conforms to what our culture sees as desirable, the more
the body is worth. Consequently girls, and the women they
become, find that their self-worth depends on how they look,
rather than who they are and what they want to be. Studies show
that children's self-esteem, especially young girls', is related to
body weight and body image.

To counteract this pressure, we need to teach children they are
worthy, based on their inner being, no matter what their body
looks like, and that bodies come in different shapes and sizes.
They need to know that they are sacred beings to be honored and
respected and listened to. They need to know that they have
brains, hearts, and souls that are full of life, intelligence, intuition, and love. They need to know that each of them is special
and necessary to our world, and has gifts to give that only they
possess.

*If there is one thing I could say to parents, it is that you
might think your kids are too young to learn about this issue. But*

they're not. You need to find dances and stuff from other cultures, like African or belly dance classes that worship all sizes and shapes, so that they can see all kinds of bodies moving and living. Get your kids involved with art or dance programs where they get to cultivate talents that don't have anything to do with how they look. That's what they need encouragement in.

— Jody

In order to really teach our children self-esteem, we need to concentrate on the very spirit of our kids. We need to encourage their creativity and support them in their interests. This will allow them to find out for themselves their own self-worth and what they came into this world to do. Teaching them to value their creative self, their own spirit, is a lesson they won't forget, even as they go through all the ups and downs of teenage years and beyond. It is critical that we, as the guardians of these young spirits, teach them that their worth as human beings is based on the inside instead of the outside.

Help Your Child Identify, Express, and Resolve Feelings

All my fears were rolled into one fear — I'm fat.

— Maggie

Many individuals with eating disorders use food, dieting, or the obsession with food and weight as a calming device to cope with difficult, uncomfortable feelings like anger, sadness, or loneliness. Helping your children to identify what they are feeling and to express their feelings in a healthy way can reduce their need to depend on external sources, such as food, alcohol, and drugs, to cope.

It is not unusual for a woman or girl to have no other feeling but the feeling of being fat. The truth is that every female knows what that means, even though fat is not a feeling. But we as women, have learned that when we are unhappy, overwhelmed, sad, confused, or uncomfortable, the feeling of "fat" is a very real feeling. Many people store their emotional pain in their bodies. They focus on their fat as being the source of their pain. They have the unrealistic expectation that if they lose weight, their problems will be solved. The pain they have stored in their bodies does not go away with the fat. In fact, the pain stays right where they've stored it until it is addressed and processed as a feeling. Eating, not eating, and changing our body size are ways of directing our attention away from the real pain that needs to be addressed. We create the more comfortable problem of an eating disorder in order to avoid dealing with the more uncomfortable feelings we are holding in our bodies. We need to teach our children ways of coping with problems that don't include changing the shape or size of their bodies. We need to teach them how to identify, express, and resolve their feelings.

Sometimes I don't know what else to do but eat. And then I feel better for awhile and then I feel worse. Even though I know it won't really work to just eat and eat, I still do.

— Cece

Overeating, undereating, and obsessing about food are ways to cope with overwhelming and painful feelings. So are alcohol or drug abuse. Parents can help their kids learn to take care of these feelings in ways that are loving and not destructive to the self. This takes time, patience, and a willingness to struggle through some strong emotions. When kids learn that their feelings are just their feelings and they won't die if they feel them, they are much more capable of handling the tough issues of growing up without turning to a substance or an obsession to numb them out. Our children's acting out is a cry for help. We need to answer that cry with understanding and the ability to listen and accept their feelings.

BE AN ACTIVIST IN YOUR COMMUNITY

Ever since I was little I had the idea that fat is bad, fat people are lazy, and fat people eat too much. But since I recovered from my own eating disorder, I've learned that our culture puts an idea in our heads of what beauty is and how we take that as the "law." I learned that there is fat discrimination and fat phobia, where people who are fat naturally are persecuted. On TV they are made fun of and shown to be lazy. This was really hard to get over because I was taught to view people in a certain way even though it is not necessarily that way at all. Now I see a connection between racism, sexism, and fatism. Fat people are left feeling real bad about themselves. They feel like they are too fat, too lazy, they eat too much, and they've done it all to themselves. This is not true. Fat people are just people. Everyone is terrified of being fat because no one wants to deal with the prejudice of it. I almost starved to death because I was so afraid of being fat.

— Vanessa

Take a stand against fatism by creating a weight-neutral/body-positive environment in your home, school, and community. Educate others about the reality that people come in all shapes and sizes, and none of them is better or worse than others. Many times we, as adults, have to look at and overcome our own prejudices before we can teach our children. But if we are willing to take the challenge, we will make this world a much better place not only for our children, but also for ourselves and for all of humankind.

Don't let your kids get away with looking down on people for their physical appearance.

— Jen

Work to bring comprehensive and effective prevention programs into your child's school. There are many new prevention programs that are being created for elementary and high schools (see Resources: The Body Positive), including educational lectures, screening, peer-support groups, peer education groups, teacher training, and referral networks for treatment.

NOTES

1 Mellin, L., et al., "A Longitudinal Study of the Dietary Practices of Black and White Girls Nine and Ten Years Old at Enrollment," *Journal of Adolescent Health*, 1991, pp. 27–37.

2 Shisslak, C. M., M. Crago, and L. S. Estes, "The Spectrum of Eating Disturbances," *International Journal of Eating Disorders*, 18 (3), 1995, pp. 209–19.

Resources

RECOMMENDED READING

Andersen, Arnold, Leigh Cohn, and Thomas Holbrook. *Making Weight: Men's Conflicts with Food, Weight, Shape & Appearance.* Carlsbad, Calif.: Gürze Books, 2000.

Bell, Ruth. *Changing Bodies, Changing Lives: A Book for Teens on Sex and Relationships.* New York: Random House, 1981.

Carlip, Hilary. *Girl Power: Young Women Speak Out.* New York: Warner Books, 1995.

Cooke, Kaz. *Real Gorgeous.* New York: Norton, 1996.

Edut, Ophira (ed.). *Adios, Barbie.* Seattle: Seal Press, 1998.

Gray, Heather, and Samantha Phillips. *Real Girl, Real World: Tools for Finding Your True Self.* Seattle: Seal Press, 1998.

Hirschmann, Jane, and Carol Munter. *When Women Stop Hating Their Bodies.* New York: Fawcett Columbine, 1995.

Nichter, Mimi. *Fat Talk: What Girls and Their Parents Say about Dieting.* Cambridge: Harvard University Press, 2000.

Normandi, Carol, and Laurelee Roark. *It's Not about Food: End Your Obsession with Food and Weight.* New York: Putnam, 1998.

Shandler, Sara. *Ophelia Speaks: Adolescent Girls Write about Their Search for Self.* New York: HarperCollins, 1999.

Wolfe, Naomi. *The Beauty Myth.* New York: William Morrow & Co, 1991.

VIDEOS

Body Talk: Teens Talk about Their Bodies, Eating Disorders and Activism. Produced by The Body Positive, 1999, Berkeley, Calif. *Body Talk* is an award-winning twenty-eight-minute video on body acceptance issues for twelve- to eighteen-year-old girls and boys. This documentary focuses on girls and boys with diverse body sizes, ethnic, and socioeconomic backgrounds. In it, teens discuss the messages they receive from media, family, and friends about their bodies and eating patterns, and their resulting struggles. They talk about how they resist and change, and how they heal. To order, contact The Body Positive (see Organizations).

ORGANIZATIONS

American Anorexia/Bulimia Association, Inc.
165 West 46th Street, Suite 1108
New York, NY 10036
(212) 575-6200
Web site: www.aabainc.org

A national nonprofit organization of concerned members of the public and health-care industry dedicated to the prevention and treatment of eating disorders through education, advocacy, and research.

Beyond Hunger, Inc.
P.O. Box 151148
San Rafael, CA 94914
(415) 459-2270
Web site: beyondhunger.org

A nonprofit organization founded by the authors of *Over It*, which provides support groups, workshops, and education for individuals with eating disorders.

The Body Positive
1115 Evelyn Avenue
Albany, CA 94706
(510) 841-9389
Web site: thebodypositive.org

A nonprofit organization whose mission is to reduce the suffering caused by preoccupation with our culture's unrealistic beauty ideals, through conducting eating disorder prevention workshops, producing videos, and supporting youth peer leaders in their work to promote body acceptance.

Eating Disorder Awareness and Prevention, Inc. (EDAP)
603 Stewart Street, Suite 803
Seattle, WA 98101
(206) 382-3587
Web site: www.edap.org

A national nonprofit organization dedicated to increasing the awareness and prevention of eating disorders through education and community activism.

WEB SITES

aabainc.org
See American Anorexia/Bulimia Association above.

about-face.org
A media literacy organization that combats negative and distorted images of women.

beyondhunger.org
See Beyond Hunger above.

bodypositive.com
A Web site that provides information and resources about positive body image.

thebodypositive.org
See The Body Positive listing under Organizations.

dadsanddaughters.org
A Web site whose mission is to strengthen relationships with daughters and transform the pervasive messages that value daughters more for how they look than who they are.

edap.org
See EDAP organization above.

overcomingovereating.com
A Web site committed to curing compulsive overeating and achieving self-acceptance no matter what your size.

somethingfishy.org
Everything you need to know about eating disorders: information, resources, and links.

Index

About Beyond Hunger

Carol and Laurelee founded Beyond Hunger, a nonprofit organization, after recovering from their own eating disorders. They wanted to create a program that incorporated the philosophies that helped them, including intuitive eating, emotional processing, and body acceptance. Beyond Hunger offers support groups, workshops and education for adults and teens with eating disorders and body image disturbances.

If you would like information on Carol and Laurelee's adult book *It's Not About Food,* or the audiotape of visualizations in this book, please contact Beyond Hunger.

Beyond Hunger relies on grants and individual donations to operate and to provide scholarships for those individuals who cannot pay for services. If you can help, please send your tax-deductible contribution to:

Beyond Hunger
P.O. Box 151148
San Rafael, California 94915-1148
(415) 459-2270
Come visit us at our Web site: beyondhunger.org

NEW WORLD LIBRARY

is dedicated to publishing books, audiocassettes,
and videotapes that inspire and challenge us
to improve the quality of our lives and our world.

Our books and tapes are available
in bookstores everywhere.
For a catalog of our complete library
of fine books and cassettes, contact:

New World Library
14 Pamaron Way
Novato, CA 94949

Phone: (415) 884-2100
Fax: (415) 884-2199
Or call toll-free (800) 972-6657
Catalog requests: Ext. 50
Ordering: Ext. 52

E-mail: escort@nwlib.com
Web site: www.newworldlibrary.com